BIPOLAR

How to Navigate Both Sides of a Bipolar
Relationship in Order to Achieve Stability

(The Complete Family Guide on Understanding
Bipolar Disorder)

William Collins

Published By Andrew Zen

William Collins

All Rights Reserved

Bipolar: How to Navigate Both Sides of a Bipolar Relationship in Order to Achieve Stability (The Complete Family Guide on Understanding Bipolar Disorder)

ISBN 978-1-77485-300-9

Legal & Disclaimer

The information contained in this book is not designed to replace or take the place of any form of medicine or professional medical advice. The information in this book has been provided for educational and entertainment purposes only.

The information contained in this book has been compiled from sources deemed reliable, and it is accurate to the best of the Author's knowledge; however, the Author cannot guarantee its accuracy and validity and cannot be held liable for any errors or omissions. Changes are periodically made to this book. You must consult your doctor or get professional medical advice before using any of the suggested remedies, techniques, or information in this book.

TABLE OF CONTENTS

Introduction

This book provides practical steps and strategies which will enable those who is suffering from a dangerous condition like bipolar disorder to live a normal , normal life. Many people might even ask whether this is even feasible. The answer is, provided that certain important decisions are made and followed.

Before all else, it should be insistent that it is not in any way and currently not intended to be used to replace medical professional advice. It is highly recommended that a qualified medical professional is aware of the situation and be able to monitor it in the event of an urgent need for a more traditional treatment using medicines or, regardless every effort the condition has begun to get more severe.

The most crucial action to take is to study, comprehend and be aware of the signs when they first show up. Learn about the disorder, its specifics, what triggers it and what to do in order to mitigate the situation and do not allow it to take over your everyday life and lead you to institutionalization, imprisonment or even death.

Bipolar disorder should not be dismissed lightly or undervalued. It is a self-destructing disorder that, if left untreated, has serious consequences which range from suicidal behavior and eventually suicide, severe criminality at all levels and eventually incarceration and the establishment of psychiatric care that can be an ordinary hospital or prison. It doesn't get better with age. If you don't take care of it, the condition is likely to get more severe.

A factor as crucial as the ability to recognize, learn and comprehend what is the right diagnosis. The condition is often misinterpreted with other illnesses such as personality, cyclothymic and the attention-deficit disorder. All of them may co-exist or be a part of bipolar disorders, but they may also be distinct conditions. This is the primary reason to seek guidance of a qualified medical expert. In the event that the diagnoses are wrong, and the treatment is not effective, it will not provide the desired and needed results.

Bipolar disorder is curable in certain circumstances. It has been proven that biological and genetic factors can make individuals vulnerable to the effects of troublesome childhood (especially by way of problems with child abuse) and a home environment that is of a turbulent nature. Prevention also concentrates on the most likely cause of nearly every kind of illness that is stress.

Another aspect to take into account when dealing with BPD is the fact that there is a significant percentage of recurrence that is up to 40% in cases that have recovered. It is a sign that patients who are suffering from the disorder must be monitored regularly for their condition in order to avoid repeat relapse.

However, as it is said the most crucial of all actions is to acknowledge the existence of an issue. The people who are in the immediate vicinity aren't necessarily contributing to the problem by continually focusing on the abnormal behavior, and often by reprimanding those who are guilty of the behavior. This is the worst option for someone who suffers from BPD.

If the person who suffers is not seeking a solution, then the treatment are ineffective or only just partially efficient. If you're suffering from BPD You must be determined to improve your condition. All else is the process of learning how to get it done.

Chapter 1: Understanding Bipolar Disorder

Bipolar disorders are more prevalent than you think. As we mentioned, about 30 million people across the globe suffer from this condition. Recent research indicates that as many as 8 million Americans suffer from this illness.

What specifically is bipolar disorder? Bipolar disorder can be described as a psychological disorder that manifests as depressive and manic symptoms. Though studies indicate that about eight million Americans suffer from this condition but the reliability of these figures is in doubt since the majority of people suffering from bipolar disorder are not seeking assistance.

What happens to the brain when you suffer from bipolar disorder? Think of the frontal part of your brain as the judgement and decision-making centers. It's like your brakes. It is the part of your brain that instructs your body to stop, there is sufficient. Your frontal lobe signals that you should slow down and consider carefully before making a decision. The amygdala on the contrary, is situated in the frontal lobe. This little portion of your brain functions as the emotional center of your. In manic episodes, your brain does not have a brake and the amygdala gets active. It becomes more difficult to control your emotions and thoughts. This is why those who experience mood swings feel irritable and, at times, extremely creative.

In depression, everything inside the frontal lobes is blocked. This means that nothing is being released. The amygdala also is turned down. If you're feeling depressed, you're in apathy and don't want to leave the house. You're not motivated to do anything.

Depressive and manic episodes can be a long-lasting event lasting for days, hours, weeks, or months. Bipolar disorder sufferers can undergo periods of depression and depressive episodes. This means that within a calendar year, people suffering from bipolar disorder usually go through four cycles.

The majority of bipolar patients begin to experience symptoms of bipolar disorder in their teens and into their the early 20s. The majority of people suffering from the condition are diagnosed before the age of 25.

The Reasons

Bipolar is a complicated disorder that can be a bit complicated. Indeed, the majority experts in the field of mental health see Bipolar to be the most complex of the conditions. The disorder is characterized by a variety of causes, which include:

Genetic Causes

As with many mental health problems bipolar disorder can be found in the family. The disorder is more prevalent for those with parents or siblings affected by this condition. Studies have shown that people who have parents with bipolar disorders have a 25% risk of developing this disorder in their 20s.

Chemical imbalances and Neurotransmitters in the Brain

Neurotransmitters (serotonin dopamine GABA glutamate, dopamine) are brain-related chemicals that play an important part for the development and progression of moo0d conditions like bipolar disorder. A chemical imbalance could trigger this condition.

Biology-related The causes

Researchers believe intracellular dysfunction could be a cause of bipolar disorder. The brain's circuits may be damaged and result in mood issues. Numerous studies suggest that hormonal issues could contribute to this condition.

Environmental Factors

A life-threatening event can cause a mood onset in someone who is susceptible genetically to suffer from bipolar disorder.

If, for instance, your father has bipolar disorder and you divorce him or lose an employment opportunity can trigger depression episodes.

The use of drugs such as amphetamine (e.g. Ecstasy) can trigger mania too. Certain health experts also believe that diet pills, prescription and over the drug products for thyroid and excessive consumption of caffeine can result in manic episodes.

Stress can induce the cycle of depression and mania for those who are prone to this condition.

Risk Factor

There are many factors in the environment and health that could trigger the creation of bipolar disorder which include:

Stressful periods for long time

A loved one's death

The emotional impact of these incidents can be seen in sexual and physical abuse

Alcoholism

Drug Abuse

Obsessive Compulsive Disorder

Divorce and relationship issues

The responsibilities that come with it, such as taking care of an elderly family member who is sick

Childhood trauma

Bipolar disorder also often occurs in conjunction with these diseases:

Anxiety disorders

Post-traumatic stress disorder

ADHD or Attention Deficit Hyperactivity Disorder. ADHD

Heart Disease

Thyroid Problems

Obesity

Substance Abuse

The signs of Manic Episodes

As previously mentioned, people who suffer from bipolar disorder have both depressive and manic episodes. Here are the signs of manic episodes.

1.Strong feelings of Invincibility

People with bipolar disorder typically feel invincible. They believe that they are able to achieve everything. This is why they are prone to high-risk behavior like participating in extreme sports.

2.Mood Swings

Bipolar disorder sufferers frequently experience mood swings as this disorder can cause manic and depression symptoms. Bipolar patients typically go through periods of positive moods and depressive periods, as well as despair.

The depressive and manic phases of bipolar disorder may vary from a few days to several months.

Patients with bipolar disorder may can also suffer from what is known as hypomania. It's a buffer state and is characterized by manic-like episodes that are mild and don't interfere with the patient's lifestyle.

3.Euphoria

When a person is in a manic stage typically, patients to feel euphoric. Patients in the manic stage of bipolar disorder typically feel a high level of joy and a sense of achievement. They take on projects that are goal-oriented which make them feel that they're invincible in their pursuit of their objectives. People suffering from bipolar disorder experience "high" when they experience hypomanic or manic episodes. They're content even in a stressful or unlucky circumstances.

4.Rapid Speech

During manic episodes bipolar disorder sufferers talk quickly. They are able to talk for long periods of time, however they cannot follow a specific train of thinking.

5.Racing Thoughts

Patients with bipolar disorder are often plagued by racing thoughts. If you're suffering from an episode of manic there will be many thoughts in within your mind. They keep going around and around. It's like all the things you've memorized throughout your life are flashing across your head. It's as if there are twenty songs playing in your head simultaneously and you're unable to distinguish everything. It's all of sounds all at the same all at once.

6.Restlessness

The symptom of restlessness is common associated with manic episode. If you're having the symptoms of a manic episode it's like you're awash of energy. It's impossible to stay for long periods of time. It's like being the ball that bounces around.

7.Feelings of Grandioseness

Delusions of grandeur are typical when you are experiencing manic episodes. People who are manic often believe they are destined to fulfill a purpose in the world. They often believe that they are a kind of royal. For instance, they could believe that they were likely to become one day the president in the United States. Certain manic individuals might have an overinflated feeling of significance. In manic episodes, some bipolar patients may feel they're instrumental in the achievement of world peace or in the development of an effective cure to AIDS.

8.Lack of Sleep

Bipolar disorder sufferers rarely fall asleep during intense episodes. They'll stay up late researching, writing, or sometimes even watching TV.

9.Reckless Behaviour

The people who suffer from manic episodes tend to engage in reckless behaviors like gambling, unprotected sex sexual relations with multiple partners, and impulse shopping sprees. In the end, they are fired or get pregnant, develop HIV and accrue an enormous amount of credit card debt.

In manic episodes, those who suffer from bipolar disorder have an elevated self-esteem. They often make poor investment decisions. It is common for them to start businesses out of a whim.

Signs of depression episodes

In addition to manic episodes, patients with bipolar disorder may also suffer from depressive episodes. Here are a few symptoms of depression they encounter:

Feelings of despair and sadness

Bipolar depression is characterised by overwhelming feelings of despair and sadness. If you're depressed, you are depressed and feel despairing. There's nothing is possible to do in order to help your situation.

Weight Gain or Appetite Changes

Depressed individuals typically eat less or excessively. This causes them to either shed weight or gain weight quickly.

Irritability

Depression sufferers tend to be irritable, and can become angry over minor things such as long lines or the storekeeper's tone of voice.

Self-Loathing

People with depression experience strong feelings of guilt and desperation. They lack self-esteem. They don't believe they deserve love, happiness or respect.

Hypersensitivity

People with depression are usually hypersensitive. They can easily be offended, and easily angry or defensive when they are criticized. They are also easily provoked.

Unscrupulous behavior

The tendency to be reckless is prevalent in the manic phase. But, it's frequent during the depression phase. People with depression frequently engage in escapist activities such as gambling addiction and substance abuse, as well as dangerous sporting activities or reckless driving.

Problems with Concentration

Depressed people are often unable to concentration. They are unable to focus on a particular task. Their productivity is affected because of this.

Tiredness as well as Lack of Energy

When you're depressed it's easy to feel that you lack the motivation to get out of bed. Therefore, you stay at home and watch the television.

A lack of interest in daily Activity

People who are depressed often have no the desire to engage in everyday activities, like taking a bath. They aren't interested in things that matter to them. They don't find joy in the activities they were used to enjoying, like shopping, sports or even sexual sex.

As previously mentioned, individuals with bipolar disorder have in the average four cycles of depression as well as manic episodes in the course of one year.

Different types of Bipolar Disorder

Bipolar I

To be diagnosed with bipolar disorder, they has to have at minimum one manic episode during his or her lifetime. Manic episodes are an intensely elevated mood that can disrupt one's daily life. It's characterized by extreme excitement as well as euphoria and energy. But, it can also become out of control. It can cause anger, irritability and even aggression. It may also result in an obsessional and reckless behaviors. Unskilled decision-making is one of the most frequent signs of manic depression.

During manic phases, individuals who suffer from bipolar disorder are prone to be aggressive, like verbal and physical attacks. Manic episodes generally affect the ability of a person to think about the implications that their choices have. These episodes of mania could ruin a person's life. Individuals experiencing mania could lose all their savings, leave their job or indulge in a spending excessive spending spree.

Bipolar II

It's like bipolar I. Bipolar II sufferers experience cycles of highs and lows. However, the difference is that people who suffer from bipolar II don't have an affliction called mania. The condition they experience is hypomania. It is an afflicted type of mania or hyperactivity. The manic episodes experienced by those suffering from bipolar II are typically manifested as psychomotor agitation, thoughts of flight, high self-esteem, and participation in activities that are enjoyable. The sole difference between hypomania as well as manic episodes is that those who suffer from hypomania are able to perform normal. They are still able to attend work or go to school.

Rapid Cycling

The people who suffer from this type of bipolar disorder typically suffer from four or more bouts of depression and mania each year. Research has shown that ten to 20 percent of those with bipolar disorder experience rapid cycles.

Cyclothymia

It is a mild disorder of mood. Patients with this disorder have mild manic and depressive symptoms.

Diagnosis

Medical tests are usually conducted by doctors particularly if the symptoms are affecting your daily routine. Doctors may request urine and blood tests to ensure that the condition isn't due to physical ailments like thyroid problems. The symptoms could be the result of a certain medications, so it is important to run medical and physical tests.

After the medical test and examinations, the general doctor will send the patient to psychiatrists to conduct a mental health assessment. Doctors typically ask patients questions regarding the symptoms and how they can affect your life. Doctors can also confirm whether bipolar disorder runs in the family.

Here's the list of criteria doctors employ to evaluate bipolar disorder:

Sleep is not necessary.

Ideas are flying around.

Race-related thoughts

There is no need for assistance

Rapid speech

Self-esteem is inflated

Psychomotor agitation

Participation in a variety of risk-taking behaviours

Energy consumption is reduced

The thoughts of suicide or death

Feelings of guilt and feeling unworthy

Feelings of feeling of

Problems with thinking and making decisions

When conducting mental examinations for bipolar disorders, doctors frequently inquire about patient's feelings and experiences. This can help them determine the severity of the condition.

Bipolar disorder is a serious condition that could ruin your life. If you're suffering from any of the above symptoms You must see your doctor immediately.

Chapter 2: Natural Products which can fight Bpd

For those who don't trust or don't want to pursue the conventional medical procedures There are natural remedies which can prove very beneficial in the treatment of BPD. It is suggested that prior to making use of any of the herbal remedies and oils listed be consulted with the medical professional as certain of them could cause adverse consequences. Here's what can be used in the treatment of bipolar disorder:

1)St. John's Wort

It is a well-known antidepressant herb. In the manic phase of the disorder, anti-depressants of any kind are not to be used. There is also a question with dosage as over use can cause the manic phase to begin. Avoid using before consulting with your physician.

2.) Flaxseed oil

It is also a type of natural antidepressant that contains alpha-linolenic acids (ALA). It's ideal when used in conjunction with conventional medical products that treat people suffering from anxiety triggered by bipolar disorder. It is not thought of as an appropriate treatment option, however the research that has been conducted shows that it can be extremely beneficial when used in conjunction with traditional medical treatments.

3) Ginseng

The herb is very beneficial in improving attention, memory levels, and focus. It is suggested to those who, following a depression episode, they experience fatigue and fatigue.

4)Gingko Biloba

This is an extract of the ginko plant and enhances memory functions and also acts as an antioxidant that aids in brain's circulation. The best results can be achieved when the herb is consumed throughout the depression phase and over a period of between eight and twelve weeks.

5) Black Cohosh

Also called black snakeroot or Squaw root. It is a depressant to the nervous system as well as is a sedative, as well as anti-inflammatory. It can be useful for an extended period of time, but this should be discussed with your attending physician since prolonged use may cause liver issues.

6) Valerian Root

It is a powerful sedative, which is also employed for treating different anxiety conditions. If used regularly, it can create an overall sense of peace and decreases stress causes. It's also very beneficial to those who experience sleep issues and headaches.

7) Licorice

This herb helps in hormonal production inside the brain. BPD sufferers should consume one cup of licorice tea every day. It's the most effective way to treat the depression aspect in bipolar disorders.

8) Passionflower

The primary benefit of passionflower is its ability to balance the levels of neurotransmitters within the brain. The sedative properties of the plant are helpful in the manic phase of BPD and also to combat insomnia. One of the side effects of the consumption of passionflower is that it upsets the stomach.

As is evident, there are plenty of natural substances that can assist sufferers of bipolar disorder in its various stages. However, this is only the beginning of the puzzle. In the chapters that flow, you will discover the additional elements that result in the result of the overcome = BPD.

Chapter 3: The What Causes

There are a variety of reasons and triggers that can cause Bipolar Disorder.However,

the precise causes of bipolar disorder are currently unknown.Bipolar disorders is more likely to result from a mix of factors. factors.Listed below are a few

Factors that influence or cause bipolar disorder in those affected by the disease.

Factors that may intensify symptoms or coexist with symptoms:

*Immune System/Autoimmune Disorder

*Neurotransmitters

*ADHD, also known as Attention Deficit Disorder and Hyperactivity Disorder

"Extreme anxiety" or anxious disorders.When children exhibit this symptom they might have fewer visits in the hospitals.

*Substance abuse and opium

Environmental Issues/Dramatic Life Changes. For instance, the loss of a family member or friend, and loss of wealth (home or car, unemployment, money etc.)

High-stress situations

*Suffering from other illnesses like cancer or obesity

*Seasonal Adverse Disorder (SAD)

*Genetics

*Cognitive Dysfunction

Genetics

Genetics play an important part in bipolar disorder.

Bipolar disorder usually runs within families. Certain studies have suggested that individuals with certain genes are more likely to suffer from bipolar disorder than those with other genes. Children who have an adult or sibling with bipolar disorder are significantly more likely to be affected by the disorder, as compared to children without any family background that has bipolar disorder. But, the majority of children who have an ancestry of bipolar disorder do not suffer from the disorder.

In twin studies in twin studies, the twin of a person who suffers from bipolar disorder does not necessarily develop the illness.Even when both twins share the same genetic profile.

Research suggests that other influences than genes may be acting upon the patient's genetics to trigger the disorder. Most likely the environment and biological factors hormonal imbalances, chemical imbalances in the brain are all responsible for the cause.

However, scientists are unable to understand the way these elements interact to trigger bipolar disorder.

Cognitive Dysfunction

The effect of weaker cognitive function is an acknowledged factor in schizophrenia, but researchers are now beginning to link this to bipolar disorder.

Cognitive impairment has been linked to bipolar symptoms such as rapid shifts in thought and lack of concentration and memory loss that are common in manic and depressive episodes.

Findings of diminished cognition during extreme or intense mood episodes are not uncommon.

However, what's most shocking is the findings of persistent cognitive impairment in bipolar patients that is the euthymic (normal non-depressed, moderately positive).The only difference is that the cognitive impairment is more severe when patients suffer from schizophrenia, compared to bipolar disorder.

Neurotransmitters

The brain utilizes neurotransmitters to send messages to the nervous system as well as other brain regions. Neurotransmitters are crucial to the functioning in the brain. The loss of neurotransmitters (chemical messengers that are found in the brain) may also contribute to the development of bipolar disorder. It is a genetic disorder. neurotransmitter dysfunction can appear to disappear, but it is then brought back by external factors or stressors.

Immune System

Infections caused by bacteria or viruses may also play a part in the development of bipolar disorder.Experts have found a link between a number of

Brain infections have been recognized as the reason for depressive and manic episodes.

Studies have shown that people who receive treatment for a serious infection have a 62% higher risk be diagnosed with mood disorders than those who have not contracted an infection in the first place.

Stress

Another cause of the bipolar disorder are stress, as well as other mental illnesses.

Stress can exacerbate depression and mania episodes The need to keep the stress level under control crucial, given the various environmental factors that can easily trigger stress.

The Seasonal Affective Disorder (SAD)

Some people experience mood swings and other manic signs in colder weather. The symptoms can appear slowly or may begin to manifest in a single day.

As the warmer seasons are approaching the symptoms start to fade gradually and then remain in Remission.

This condition is also known as SAD, also known as Seasonal Affective Disorder or SAD.

People suffering from SAD can experience depressive episodes or bipolar disorder in winter, and the episodes disappear in summer.

SAD has been linked to imbalances in biochemicals within the brain, which are triggered by with the changes in the environment that occur during the winter months, such as fewer hours of daylight hours and lack of sunlight. As the seasons change, our human body alters its circadian rhythm. this can disrupt our daily routines.

Attention Deficit Hyperactivity Disorder (ADHD)

ADHD is a frequent occurrence that is common among people who suffer from bipolar disorder.This can also cause a confusion and rapid shifts in thought.

Adults who suffer from ADHD may also have bipolar disorder, which demands careful evaluation to identify and treat both disorders.

Bipolar disorder is most likely to develop in a large proportion of children suffering from ADHD. The onset of bipolar disorder is usually due to the growth of ADHD. At first, ADHD and bipolar disorder aren't easy to tell between the two. The prescription medications for ADHD which contain stimulants can cause a rise in moodiness.

Particularly, in those who are at risk of developing bipolar disorder.

Anxiety Disorders and Extreme Anxiety

Anxiety disorders are common among people with bipolar disorder.

Anxiety disorders are often triggered when worries or anxieties last over weeks, days, months or even years.These fears persist despite

There is no logical or rational explanation.

Anxiety is a common occurrence in the deep depressions and extreme highs in bipolar disorder. Sometimes, it even triggers symptoms.

It's easy to become nervous when confronted with stressful daily chores and responsibilities.

People suffering from bipolar disorder who suffer from excessive anxieties are likely to be involved in this type of intense worry and more likely to commit suicide behavior.However people who have bipolar disorder, but don't suffer from severe anxiety or an anxiety disorder are less at risk of engaging in suicidal behaviors.

Substances and Opium Abuse

Opium and other substances can increase symptoms, but it is common among people with bipolar disorder.

People with bipolar disorder are at a higher risk of consuming substances.

Marijuana and alcohol are among the most commonly used drugs among bipolar patients.

The reason could be a change in the neural reward system in ADHD people. The result is that the diagnosis and management of ADHD more challenging and more serious addiction issues usually being addressed first due to their higher risks.

Chapter 4: Recognition

Depression, just like mania, is the most painful of experiences. This is due to the fact that during these times people are aware there is something wrong. In the majority of cases, many of these emotions are accompanied by anxiety. They can get too intense for the individual that they can leave someone in a state of shock in awe, wondering where they did something wrong. In certain instances there are instances of intense fatigue and anxiety that are the primary indicator that is bipolar disorder.

Affects and signs of the depressed condition of Bipolar disorder

One of the most obvious signs of someone who is suffering from depression or bipolar disorder can be seen in that, in most instances they feel a constant sense of depression, sadness and anxiety. They are often depressed about numerous things, including eating, sexual activity and work, among others. Even though the individual may have taken enough rest, they usually find themselves exhausted and tired. When they do try to sleep, it is difficult and, when they do sleep, they usually awake early or sleep too much. People with depression typically have a problem with abnormal behavior, such as a reduced or an increased appetite, which eventually alters their weight. They may not be able to concentrate on their work for long, and when they have to make decisions regarding their job they're unsure. This leads to emotions of shame and anger that affects their self-esteem. This low self-esteem that can cause individuals to think of suicide.

However in the case of mania, or the less severe type of mania, which is known as hypomania, it's usually not as obvious to the individual suffering from the condition. It is due to the fact that it is typically connected with extreme feelings of joy. The great thing about mania is that it's not common for them to be diagnosed for prolonged durations of time. The reason for this is that the signs are very apparent. The symptoms can include anxiety, a lack of focus when it comes to their interests, over-talking and insomnia. This is what frequently make the others around them feel like the person is acting in a way that is not normal.

In the case of hypomania in which the patient has less energy, this may go undiagnosed for long durations of time. This is due to the fact that in many instances, this type of disorder is typically referred to as uncharacteristic for the individual. Most of the time, if family members are observant to observe, they may have noticed certain episodes in which the individual has a few mild highs. This is due to the person's mood can be uncommonly positive and optimistic.

Signs and symptoms of mania/elation in Bipolar disorder

Most of the time, when the patient suffers from mania, there's an underlying change in their emotions that can affect the way they think in an overly optimistic manner. It is common for them to feel that they feel like they're at the top of their game and are way better than they have ever been or even better than the norm. But, on certain days, they might be irritable and touchy. They typically experience a strong desire to be energetic that causes them to complete a lot of work, without taking a break. It is possible that they are busy, distracted and agitated. This is often accompanied by a lot of tension in the brain such that their minds are unable to be turned off easily.

If they are in this way, they tend to move from one topic to the next. They have unrealistic expectations regarding their capabilities, which can lead to poor judgement in their decision-making processes. In contrast to those with depression, those with mania usually exhibit an excessively high level of interest in activities that are enjoyable. They may engage in sexual relations as well as alcohol as well as new ventures, illicit/street drugs and music, religion and art among other. In addition they tend to be aggressive, insistent, and aggressive and display a active behaviour. When they are in this mode they are unable to recognize the need for changes because they believe there's nothing wrong with them.

Are Bipolar disorder more that just a mood shift?

Did you have the knowledge the fact that Bipolar illness is much more than just a mood shift? The most important aspect to be aware of is that bipolar disorder can be treated as a medical condition. Like we said earlier the moods of someone suffering from this condition can range from depression to mania and reverse. These changes in moods that typically are lasting for several hours, days, weeks, or even months.

Bipolar disorder is a problem that affects more than two million adults, particularly those in the United States. Like other mental disorders like depression, it is often a major affect on partners, families members and colleagues at work and also friends. The illness isn't gender specifically, and that is why there's an equal amount of women and men who suffer from the illness. It is also common in all races, ethnicities, ages and an individual's social class.

People often mistake bipolar disorder with depression. In reality that, according to research, there is evidence to point towards a clear distinction between bipolar disorder and clinical depression. This is because the symptoms and signs of both conditions are similar, especially during the depressive phase of bipolar disorder. The mood swings that accompany bipolar disorder typically range from extreme levels of energy to deep despair. These extreme shifts in moods that can cause significant disruption to routine activities, thereby separating the disease from normal fluctuations in mood.

Contrary to those who suffer from clinical depression those who are identified as having bipolar disorders typically have lows and highs in the disease. The highs are called mania/euphoria, while the lows are typically called depression. Certain climate conditions, such as autumn and winter, reports revealed that the majority of bipolar disorder sufferers often exhibit signs of depression. However, in the spring, many suffer from symptoms of mania, or a milder type of mania known as hypomania.

What are the complication with bipolar disorder?

Bipolar disorder sufferers typically live a challenging life that is a consequence of their behavior and personality. Most of the time, they suffer from a challenging social life and are often seen as the cause of problems in families. This is often the result of someone in a heightened state of being so domineering insistent demanding, aggressive and demanding. Family conflicts can result in marital breakups. There are times when a person exhibits excessive spending habits, an increased sexual desire that leads the couple into sexual affairs outside of marriage, or abusive and aggressive behavior with other people. Most of the time, these are too much for spouses to manage and they decide to divorce even after years of a steady marriage.

Other effects could be bad school and work performance or loss of work because of a lower level of productivity at work or , even more notably an abuse of their colleagues making work a risk for everyone else. Due to their capacity to spend too much, they frequently empty their accounts of cash and can be in the process of filing for bankruptcy. Furthermore, they could take part in alcohol or illegal substances use. It is common for them to face legal issues that can range from indiscreet or aggressive behavior or making offensive remarks, ignoring traffic rules and other behaviors caused by their over-estimation of their abilities. Due to their extreme behavior individuals often become tired of them and can become isolated. The lack of social interaction in their life may lead to a feeling of guilt, self-worthlessness and depression. This lack of self-esteem that eventually leads them into a depression and leads to suicidal thoughts.

Types of Bipolar Disorder Episodes

Manic episodes are typically thought of as a specific period of continuous increase in mood. The mood, in this instance is generally agitated and depressed and lasts at least one week. One thing to keep in mind is that when a manic episode occurs at least three symptoms of mania typically manifest.

Hypomanic episodes: These are exactly like the manic episodes, with the exception of the fact that in this instance the patient does not suffer from hallucinations or illusions. Also, hypomanic episodes tend to be more mild than manic episodes. The patient isn't suffering from the typical depression mood. This is due to the fact that patients is often unable to function, and can exhibit behaviors that are not in the norm.

Major depression instances: In this scenario it is common for people to suffer for a duration that is two or more weeks. In this time, the sufferer is suffering from more than five symptoms of depression.

Mixed episodes occurs usually the case when the patient is suffering from symptoms of depression and mania each day for more than one week.

Rapid cycling The term "rapid cycling" refers to the period of time when the patient has more than four signs of hypomania, mania, mixed depression , and depression in a prolonged time of one year.

Chapter 5: Helping Others in Living a Healthy Life

Although your brain may not be in the best shape, you can aid it by making sure your entire body is. An active lifestyle is a vital treatment method. The food you eat as well as how much sleep you get significantly affect how your symptoms impact your. A lot of people who don't adhere to a routine do not adhere to healthy lifestyles. If you live a life that is unhealthy is also a source of weight gain and create depression, making symptoms more severe. A lack of consistency in your routine isn't good and following a poor one is even worse and will likely make the issue worse as time passes. Because it's only a tiny change there's no reason to not to change your routine into healthier.

Nutrition

The food you consume can influence your mood, however regardless of the fact that chocolate is an antidepressant that has been proven to work, but that doesn't mean you have to take it for granted. Food is fuel for your body , and it is a rich source of vitamins and minerals. These aid in the production of the same chemicals that your brain creates and is influenced by. Insufficient intake of the nutrients it requires and your body will not make the chemical that it needs so that your brain can feel more relaxed. For some, eating food is a way to improve their mood, however it can also lead to weight gain and unhealthy dependence on food.

Many people choose to eat sweet, sugary or fatty foods when they're feeling low due to their natural boost effect. However, these foods are very calorific and not rich in nutrients. Sugar is the most significant cause of this. It's been found to be just as addicting as other drugs because it releases opioids as well as dopamine, which makes people feeling "good". It triggers addiction with cravings and withdrawals however it can also trigger anxiety as well as the effects of hypoglycemia resulting from an uncontrollable sugar crash. Consuming products that contain sugar can trigger a similar cycle to bipolar, and should be avoided as far as you can.

Instead of filling yourself up with refined or sweet foods, opt for ones that are nutritionally rich. This includes a range of fruits, whole food items, and even vegetables. It is recommended to stay clear of alcohol too since it is basically liquid sugar along with sodas and juices. Artificial sweeteners are equally harmful as sugar, but with lower calories and should be avoided as they can cause the same dependence and instability.

Sugary and processed foods can cause inflammation. that can negatively impact the brain and how it functions and put more strain to the human body. Inflammation is also associated with an insufficient immune response and weight gain, so you should stay clear of it as much as you can.

Nutrient Therapy

An intriguing alternative treatment that came from the body's natural cravings process. Scientists are beginning to study what exactly makes us reach for the refrigerator and how these components impact the brain. Science is firmly proving that the consumption of vitamin supplements daily and certain amino acids could help to decrease symptoms since they convert into chemicals that the brain needs. Contrary to conventional medications they do not have any negative side effects and are also much less expensive.

The most sought-after supplement for people suffering from bipolar disorders includes an Omega-3 Fatty Acid. It is typically found in fish oil. Inability to make these acids is recognized in patients and is similar to the inhibition of neurotransmitter pathways that are characteristic of bipolar disorder. Two grams per day of these supplements has been proven to decrease depression by 50%.

Vitamin C along with Folic acid have been proven to be essential for those suffering from bipolar. Bipolar sufferers typically have elevated homocysteine levels. This is usually the reaction of our body when we have low amounts of folate levels and insufficient Vitamin C consumption. People who have functional decline generally have higher levels of homocysteine levels in their plasma.

Sleep

If establishing a good sleeping routine is a crucial an important aspect of managing your symptoms, it can be among the most difficult things to do for people suffering from. There are many instances that having bipolar disorder hinders people from having a regular sleep routine. A consistent sleep schedule is almost as crucial as having a steady routine. Insufficient or excessive sleep can be dangerous and could trigger swings.

Healthy sleeping habits include making a bed and waking up time that's consistent throughout the day, including weekends. The ability to "Sleep in" because you are feeling like it's often a reason to let depression habits develop. One of the most common signs of depression is that you sleep too much. So when you're planning to go to bed at a time that is reasonable, you shouldn't have to think about staying up late. Napping in the same way isn't helpful since it disrupts your sleep schedule in the evening and may result in weight increase. If you're napping you're burning less calories and have less chance to engage in activities that can help your symptoms.

Caffeine can be a major issue for a lot of people including bipolar sufferers. Avoid drinking caffeine after lunch because it can lead people to stay awake unnecessarily late. TV, laptop and mobile screens are equally disruptive and should not be used during the evening. Even though you're not consuming sugar, they can cause similar effects. Healthy sleeping habits include that you don't eat or drink immediately prior to bed, as you'll have to go to your bathroom, or to treat stomach discomfort. Do not eat anything for an hour prior to you go to bed.

Treatments

Consume multivitamins and supplements with fish oil as an alternative method of nutrition treatment. A lack of nutrients and a low intake of the essential elements required for your body to make the proper chemicals can lead to more severe symptoms. A healthy and balanced lifestyle which includes adequate sleep can help keep your body in check and help you stay in a more stable state.

Example Mark:

Mark has a very busy and difficult job. It's demanding and difficult, and he's not always eating regularly or get enough sleep. Late evenings mean that even when he does attempt to sleep, he's usually awake. He grabs a multivitamin in order to fill the gaps in his diet. He notices that he's feeling better , so it's time to think about other healthy changes. Through adjusting his routine, the man can set an ideal sleep schedule, and helps improve the mood of his. Mark is working to eat healthier and shed weight, that boosts confidence in himself. Mark is taking his medication, but he feels better than just functional.

Chapter 6: What Treatment Options Are Available?

Yes. I'm Bipolar...I take a medication to reduce excessive highs. I take a medication to reduce the lows to a minimum. I take a medication to sleep. I take a medication to combat anxiety. I don't like taking the pills but I'm also healthy." (Unknown) (Gluck, "Quotes on Bipolar")

The treatment for bipolar disorder involves psychotherapy, medication, and behavior therapy, as well as other therapies options for maintaining an active lifestyle. Medical experts have studied carefully treatments for a lengthy duration. Different types of drugs are utilized in different stages of the disease. Antipsychotic medications are utilized to treat depression. In the past, there was a lot of confusion and doubt about the efficacy of antidepressants for treating depressive patients. Lithium bicarbonate is one of the drugs which has demonstrated the greatest efficacy in stopping recrudescence. There is a lot of uncertainty regarding the effectiveness of lamotrigine, as well as other antipsychotics.

Despite the many treatment options available, many patients fall back with the disease within a year of being diagnosed. It is estimated that three-quarters of the patients who relapse to depression, or even mania, and 60% return within 2 years of diagnosis. [15]

Treatment for Manic Episode

Jonathan was uncontrollable one day. He couldn't be stopped. He was unable to sleep for the duration of one night. It was impossible to sleep while he was creating a new project for his computer job. Next day, he appeared completely deluded. He was talking at the rate of ten mile per minute. He had a gallon coffee to compensate for the sleep deprivation. When he arrived at work, people started to observe that he was chatting in a snark about work. He was not usually behaving like this. He was talking about how he was planning to get out of the job. He was fired immediately after he announced that. His coworkers were terrified of what they saw happening. They told him, "Jonathan needs help. We should communicate with Jonathan."

A number of trials were conducted during the 70s and 1980s with substances like chlorpromazine and lithium. Additionally, there were tests conducted with antipsychotic medicines. The results revealed that antipsychotic medication was the most effective drugs that can be utilized for treating severe manic episodes. This class of medications includes Olanzapine, Risperidone, as well as haloperidol (Geddes and Miklowitz, 2013,). While these drugs were proven to be effective in combating the symptoms of manic depression, those that proved long-lasting efficacy in dealing with those symptoms that are associated with mania as well as stopping relapses comprised lithium bicarbonate.

The treatment of bipolar disorder is a huge problem for both patients and doctors since a large portion of the treatment relies on the effectiveness and use of treatment. Alongside lithium, the antiepileptic drug lamotrigine, has been found to possess a"placebo effect" (Geddes and Miklowitz, 2013).Treatment of other antipsychotic medicines has been found to be beneficial to the treatment of patients suffering from bipolar disorder.

Long-term treatment of the illness

The most efficient long-term treatment to treat bipolar disorders is lithium bicarbonate that was first developed through John Cade in 1949 (Geddes and Miklowitz Geddes and Miklowitz, 2013). This drug has been used for over 50 years and there have been a few studies conducted to demonstrate its effectiveness.

However it is not always the sole treatment option for patients. In many instances lithium, it is necessary to combine with other medications to achieve efficacy as a treatment option. Lithium is a fantastic mood stabilizer. However, when dealing with other issues, such as anxiety and depression it can be very ineffective.

Antipsychotic medication is used to control the symptoms of depression and manic symptoms in bipolar patients, they're been less effective in long-term care according to research conducted by medical professionals.

Treatment for a depressive episode

Rebecca has recently been suffering with depression. Her mother passed away from cancer. She spent three weeks in the hospital while her mother was receiving last treatments for her tumor in the brain. Rebecca was devastated beyond any words. She didn't know what she should do as she'd lost much of her energy. She couldn't even get herself to work in the early morning. All she wanted was to do was sleep and not leave her the bed. Rebecca recognized that something was not right. She was aware that she was depressed and wanted to break free of it. In the next few days, Rebecca knew that she had to visit her doctor, so she saw a doctor for adjustments to her medication, and also to place her on antidepressants like Zoloft. She noticed that she was getting better as time went on, but it took some time to completely recover from the depression-related episode.

Rebecca looked for the proper type of treatment after being diagnosed with depression. She immediately went to see her doctor and stated she was suffering from depression. She did not try to overcome the depression by herself. She sought the help she required through an adjustment to her medication. After receiving the treatment she needed, Rebecca was given a program of sleep medications (melatonin) to control her circadian rhythm as well as an exercise program. Since Rebecca enjoys running she was able to take a run every time she felt depressed. She could feel much better in the event that she could handle her feelings. When she exercised and getting active, she was able overcome the issue of depression. In most cases, it's just walking for a short distance or dancing to your favorite radio station, or even talking with somebody to help you get off of your down mood and back into something that will assist you.

Rebecca recognized that she had to help those who was in need. Therefore, she was recommended by her doctor discuss her concerns with her friends and get involved in their lives, but not worry about guilt. Minor issues aren't an issue over the long term. The most important thing is to seek medical attention in the event of a need.

In Rebecca's case Rebecca She was able to seek assistance she needed by speaking with her friends and seeking their opinions on the situation which was a huge help in helping her recover from the trance of depression and despair.

Rebecca was able to schedule the opportunity to see her mentor.They had a chat over coffee and discussed her recent depression episode. Face-to-face interactions had a major impact on her. She felt much better after their conversation.

Face-to-face interactions are crucial in the recovery process from depression. While texting and messaging are commonplace in today's technology, there's nothing like having an actual conversation with somebody. Rebecca was in a position to engage in this conversation while she dealt with her circumstances.

Rebecca later became part in The Big Brother and Sister Club. She was determined to assist other people who are experiencing issues. She chose to help a young girl who has ADHD problems. It was a great way to feel happier knowing she was capable of helping people who was in need.

In order to provide her with ongoing care, Rebecca was able to assist others. Studies have proven the importance of helping other people and assisting those in need is a method to help you recover from depression-related episodes and boosts your confidence and also. [16]

Let's take a look at some of the basics that can be gleaned from this case of how to deal with depression. What are some tips or advice to deal with an episode of depression?

1. Speak to someone about your emotions. Release your feelings.

2. Give someone else a helping hand by volunteering your time and energy to an organization you are a believer in.

3. Make a connection with someone in an eatery or during lunch.

4.Ask someone to sit with you at various times during your depressive episode.

5.Take the time to take a strenuous stroll or run across the street. You'll feel instant benefits exercise and has been shown to boost your mood almost immediately, due to the chemical changes that exercise brings.

6.Meet individuals regularly for a social activity you are interested in. The group therapy you receive will help you to better deal with your feelings.

7.Talk with the pastor of an institution, a teacher or a coach about your issues.

Therapy as an Method of Treatment to treat Bipolar Disorder

Another option for treating patients suffering from bipolar disorder is psychotherapy. In psychotherapy, the patient talks to the therapist such as psychologists, to track the mood of the patient and create a treatment plan. Alongside the therapist the patient devises strategies for managing the symptoms and stress. They also discuss ways to keep a healthy and positive life style that incorporates exercises, sleep and healthy routines to follow.The therapy therapist will listen to your concerns. If you're in need of someone to vent and talk to, you can speak to your therapist. They will listen and ask you questions about your experiences, and offer you strategies to deal with your issues as a bipolar sufferer. Therapists are the one who can work with your psychiatrist when coming up with the best treatment strategy. The therapist you choose to work with will not be knowledgeable about medical or scientific study on chemical reaction. He will instead know some psychosocial strategies that will help you achieve wellness within your daily life. Discussing your issues with a therapist can help you have a healthy life free of stress. Your therapist will show you how to recognize your anxiety triggers and how to manage them to stop relapses from happening.

The Common Goals for Psychotherapy

1. Make sure you intervene early if there are warning signs of the possibility of a relapse

2.Help the patient accept the diagnosis.

3.Encourage the patient to take the medication.

4.Manage the patterns of sleep and encourage healthy habits across all aspects of your life

5.Encourage patients to steer clear of drinking alcohol and other drugs.

The Places Where Psychotherapy Isn't Working[1717

Psychotherapy may not be beneficial when there are severe signs of manic symptoms because the patient is not willing to talk to anyone during it. The patient may be in denial of the reality of the situation when he or she is in a manic episode.Psychotherapy should not be used alone in the treatment of bipolar disorder. It should be utilized alongside mood stabilizers to last in treating the condition.

Studies on psychotherapy have demonstrated that using psychotherapy in long-term treatment for patients will provide the best benefits , and will reduce the chance of the possibility of relapse. [18]

Cognitive Behavioral Therapy (CBT)

Cognitive-behavioral therapy is a form of psychotherapy which aims at changing an individual's ways of thinking and behaving , and helps people to relax. It's a form of training that helps you to be relaxed. There are numerous techniques that CBT can be utilized to help you relax, such as deep breathing techniques and techniques to train you to to sleep quickly. Certain methods of using CBT allow you to unwind at a moment's notice using muscle manipulation and other methods. However, the main thing CBT accomplishes is that it teaches the individual to be aware of their own negative and positive ways of thinking and allows them utilize them in a constructive way to achieve results that are proven.

What happens during CBT Talk Therapy?

CBT is a gruelling training program that takes between 5 or 20 sessions. each session is between 30 and 1 hour. In these sessions the therapist and you engage in talks and talk about the issues and problems in your life. They will also assist you shift habits of thinking and behavior which are harmful for your wellbeing. After identifying the root of the problem the therapist will provide you a strategy to follow and work on throughout the week. Each week , you'll be able to report back to your therapy therapist on your progress.The purpose of this type of therapy is for you to understand how to manage anxiety and stress within your daily life.

Benefits of CBT

CBT is a successful method of treating patients suffering from bipolar disorder, particularly when treatment hasn't worked.It can also be used quickly and provide you with the necessary steps to overcome episodes of depression or mania. The treatment plan outlines methods and suggestions to use throughout your life. It also allows you to create useful action plans that you can follow regardless of when your treatment is done.

Advantages of CBT

CBT is a time-consuming process and requires your full dedication to attain the desired results.It could require extra effort due to the fact that you may have tasks that your therapist has assigned you to complete, which will take up a portion amount of time. Additionally, it can cause you to feel uncomfortable because you're directly confronting your thoughts and behavior patterns. It is possible to be feeling anger, anxiety or frustration with your pattern of thinking, which could result in anxiety in your life.

The overall conclusion is that CBT could be a beneficial element of your daily routine, and you should think about it as a method of help you develop an optimistic outlook and improve in managing your mood and the symptoms that are associated with this disorder.

Family as a Type of Therapy

Families are a vital part of our lives. Family is essential especially for those suffering from bipolar disorder, it's important to have a solid family history that can aid in the treatment of the disease. Studies have proven that people who suffer from bipolar disorder who received family therapy had a 30 to 35 percent lower chance of hospitalization, relapse and lesser severe signs of bipolar disorder (Geddes and Miklowitz, 2013,). Family members' role could be problematic when there is conflicts or conflict in the household unit. It could cause issues for the mental health of a person.

Skills for communication and therapy and Interpersonal Communication.

In addition to the earlier types of therapy, there's the aspect of interpersonal communication, which has been proven to have advantages. When you're able to talk about your concerns with a trusted person or mentor you are able to get the same type of therapy that you receive from CBT or psychotherapy, since you are able to pinpoint the issue and determine the root cause. After that, you'll be able to discuss with your partner the answers to your issues. It is often beneficial to "talk things over," and you can achieve the results you're looking for. With the assistance of a coach or a person whom you trust, will get the expert advice and guidance that will benefit you, and you will be able to improve your life. It can do wonders for your life.

Group Therapy

Another option for therapy is to engage in group activities since it helps you deal with your symptoms and provide you with an enjoyable and beneficial activities to engage with others. Being with other people to discuss your concerns offers a number of proven benefits which will allow you to maximize the benefits of your treatment. Additionally, there's the power of numbers and having other people on your side will help in achieving your fitness program.

Writing as a method of Therapy

Then, writing notes of your ideas, regardless of whether it is writing in a journal or writing novels, blogging or whatever, is an effective way to communicate your inner thoughts and emotions which could cause you to behave. Sometimes, these thoughts are simply repressed inside the mind, and you must discover a way to bring your thoughts out in a constructive manner. It's not an easy task however, with careful thinking and planning, you could write down your thoughts to put your thoughts down on paper or screen. If you can see the root of what is bothering you, it is possible to think precisely about your concerns and confront them head-on using the organization and structure. This is essential to create the plan of action that will take you to the place of being healthy. It is essential to continue receiving support. Your writing may be to be used on a blog, or even in an individual journal. The writing doesn't need to be shared, except you choose to share it. Happy writing!

As you've seen there are many options to treat bipolar disorder by using different methods. Medicine is just one piece in the puzzle of bipolar management however, there are other components of a total treatment strategy. In many instances it is the usage of talk therapy, whether it's psychotherapy or CBT will be vital. However, they are not the only treatment options. Your loved ones, your interests and hobbies, as well as an individual group can provide an outlet that can give you therapy that you could not receive through psychotherapy. It is essential to have an outlet to express your emotions. This is crucial to achieving the outcome you're looking for. Being supported by other people is essential to this procedure as you cannot accomplish it by yourself. You require others to be a part of your life.Your family, your friends and your doctor, your Therapist, your group, you need all of them to be a part of your life, so be sure to seek assistance when you require it.

Chapter 7: Types Of Bipolar Disorder

There are various types of bipolar disorders, ranging from the extremes of mania and depression. The symptoms can differ in severity from mild to extreme, dependent on the type of disorder that is discussed below:

Bipolar 1

Bipolar 11

Bipolar 111

Rapid cycling

Mixed bipolar and

Cyclothymia.

All bipolar types suffer from manic-hypermanic and depressive episodes in different extents. Mania is typically characterized by

Sudden euphoria or rage

Hyperactivity

Hallucinations

Self-esteem is inflated

Race-related thoughts

Sleepiness is reduced and

The obsession with non-essential matters.

Mania is also associated with reckless behaviors like spending too much and shopping sprees that are extravagant and sexual activities that are risky or investments that are risky. It is the mild type of mania, which is characterized as euphoria , hyperactivity and. The depression component of bipolar disorder is similar to the symptoms of depression in clinical cases and mania, which includes

A persistent sadness and fatigue

The loss of interest in certain activities

Changes in eating and sleeping patterns

Inability to concentrate

An overwhelming sense of hopelessness and inadequacy and

Suicide or death thoughts.

Of the many bipolar forms The most serious type is the bipolar 1 disorder. Bipolar 1 sufferers might experience manic episodes which begin in a flash and last approximately 4 months on average. Bipolar 1 depressive episodes can last for around 6 months to 1 year. The patients might need hospitalization due to an episode of manic has become out of control, or suicidal thoughts are too intense. People get themselves into trouble because they take too much, or not taking dangers and ending up in jail or getting injured. They appear to have endless energy for doing things that are not critical.

The existence of mixed episodes that include depressive and manic symptoms can increase the risk of suicide.

Bipolar 11 disorders is milder version that is also the one most prevalent. Subjects with this disorder experience less emotions of irritability and euphoria, which are then depressive episodes with greater intensity. It can be difficult to recognize hypomania since it can manifest as a part in the persona. It can trigger severe disturbance and difficulty in with concentration. Bipolar disorder that is rapid cycling is defined by rapid alternating depression and euphoria within the span of a few minutes. The phases of depression tend to be more frequent and but are also accompanied by short periods of manic or hypomanic episodes. Anyone is affected by the bipolar disorder that is rapid and cycling. it is more common among women than men.

Bipolar 111 refers to when an emotional state or mania is caused by medications. If a patient is being treating for depression, the medication prescribed can cause manic moods. It is classified in bipolar.

When a person is diagnosed with mixed bipolar, the lows and highs of the condition typically occur in rapid succession. In this situation, hospitalization might be necessary since the sufferer might experience psychotic symptoms such as hallucinations, delusional behavior or hallucinations. There is a general belief that 20 to 70 percent of those suffering from bipolar disorder have mixed episodes, especially in the adolesence phase when the issue is first noticed.

Cyclothymia patients suffer from hypomania and suffer from moderate to mild depression. Cyclothymia patients tend to stay in touch with the world around them. The mood elevation or depression isn't too drastic. The people don't become completely depressed however, they do go through periods of depression and periods of high mood.

Chapter 8: The subject is Psychotherapy.

Since it is classified as a psychiatric disorder most people automatically link bipolar disorders with different (and frequently more extreme) forms of psychiatric disorder such as schizophrenia or even antisocial personality disorders. Here are a few of the most popular myths people have about bipolar disorder and the ways it can be controlled or managed.

Bipolars aren't able to lead normal lives.

The truth is that there are many bipolars, both diagnosed and undiagnosed who live fulfilling and happy lives, with successful careers as well as healthy familial or romantic connections. On the other hand bipolar disorder, it can be debilitating and difficult for anyone dealing with it however, with the proper treatment, appropriate handling and the full support of family members, it can be treated and a normal, fulfilling life is still feasible.

Every bipolar suffers from depression and mania in a series of phases throughout their lives

It is true that not all bipolars fall within the extreme bipolar spectrum although it is true that certain bipolars experience episodes more often and more intensely than other bipolars. But many bipolars belong to the hypomanic spectrum, with instances of manic depressive episodes which are mild enough that they're often undiagnosed and are not recognized. There are bipolars whose manic depression episodes are few and far between.

Bipolar disorder is only manifested during mood changes

It's a fact: Bipolar disorder in general impacts not just the mood of a person, but also energy levels, as well as the brain functions that allow people to focus and make informed decisions and to recall things. Bipolar disorder can also impact the sex drive of a person sleep patterns, sex drive, and self-image. It's a psychological disorder that is linked to addiction to drugs and other anxiety and personality issues, and can cause further psychological issues in the event of untreated.

The only medication that can treat bipolar disorder.

The truth is that medication plays a significant part in treating and managing bipolar patients. But, medications alone will not treat bipolar disorder. Patients require the right treatment and all the help they can receive from relatives and friends. Self-help guides can assist bipolar patients control their thoughts and manage their triggers more effectively.

Psychotherapies are available for Bipolar Disorder

As we've previously discussed the bipolar disorder is managed, but it can be a long and painful procedure for the sufferer as well as those around him.

The treatment for bipolar disorder typically involves two parts such as psychotherapy and medication. In this article we will look at psychotherapy and its role to treat bipolar disorder. Be aware, however, that even though therapy and medications can help manage bipolar disorder but it is an ongoing battle. Studies suggest that even cases that have been treated successfully exhibit signs and symptoms of the condition.

Relapse remains a possibility as well as recovering patients may experience periodic mood fluctuations however, they'll be much more manageable levels that if the condition remained untreated. Here are some types of treatments that are often prescribed for bipolar disorder sufferers.

Cognitive Behavioural Therapies are commonly employed not just for the treatment of bipolar disorder, but also for many behavioral disorders. In this type of treatment, a person is trained to understand his behaviour patterns and thoughts and tendencies and alter those that are negative, which can cause a manic depressive episode.

Psychoeducation provides bipolar patients with the understanding of their conditions and how they can be managed. It aids them to prevent or treat the condition's beginning stages by identifying the first symptoms and signs.

Family therapy is a therapy that's designed to assist a patient in coping with bipolar disorder by enlisting the help from his loved ones. It also aims to help the families of people with bipolar disorder more aware of the disorder and give all the assistance they can to assist the patient cope with his episodes and triggers. It strengthens the bonds of families and helps how to come up with strategies to deal with the situation if the patient has an episode. It can also help bridge any gaps that could have been due to the condition.

Group therapy is more of a bipolar support group patients who can share their experiences with one another and learn about the therapy methods and medications helped others.

Therapy for social rhythms is designed to help patients with bipolar disorder cope better with their interpersonal relationships and cope with social situations better. Another method is to establish routines and routines that help to avoid the onset of manic episodes.

Other Treatments

Electroconvulsive Therapy (ECT) is also known as Shock Therapy is the last resort treatment for patients who are not responding to other types of therapy or medications. ECT basically uses electric stimulation when the patient is anesthetized to ensure that he does not experience the electrical shock.

This treatment is only thirty seconds to one and a half minutes. After a short period of time the patient is able to leave the hospital, completely recuperated. It has been proven beneficial, particularly for severe manic-depressive episodes.

Hospitalization has been rarer for patients suffering from bipolar disorder in recent years. (Most patients are seen as outpatients.) It can be a last resort particularly for cases of extreme severity where there are signs of psychosis or hallucinations. It is also suggested for patients who have the history of self-harm or having suicidal thoughts in their incidents.

Lifestyle Changes

The most important aspect of psychotherapy is the ability to alter an entire set of habits for a patient, and to encourage the patient to develop certain habits that will prevent triggers of manic-depressive episodes. This includes getting enough sleep as well as resting, eating nutritious food choices, and maintaining an active life style.

The treatment of bipolar disorder is a constant battle and commitment. There's no definitive cure for bipolar disorder. even medicines must be administered regularly to avoid the appearance of severe attacks or to make them manageable. Patients can't decide to discontinue treatment or medication simply because they noticed improvements in his condition.

The treatment doesn't stop at taking medicines frequently. While medications are an important aspect of treatment for bipolar disorder there are other factors to consider like environmental factors and the support from a patient's family and friends. Experts suggest patients keep a journal every day to record not only their medications, but also their moods thoughts, emotions, and moods during treatment.

Ask for help from a professional. A consultation with an expert in psychiatry is the best option even in seemingly unimportant cases of hypomania, mania or depression. A professional can guide patients in not only guiding them through therapy but will also make sure they receive the right treatment.

Chapter 9: Causes Of Bipolar Disorder

As with other mental disorder it is possible for bipolar disorder to be explained through a myriad of causes. Numerous studies were conducted to discover the root cause of this condition. But, the bipolar disorder can't be solely attributed to one factor. Most of the time there are a variety of various factors come together to explain the cause of this disorder. Two of the most common factors the explanation of a mental disorder will be covered in this section : psychological and neurological aspects.

There are a variety of approaches in analyzing the neuro-related elements involved in bipolar disorder. You must remember that the neurological aspects are based in the body's biology. The explanation of genes, the neurophysiology, and the brain's chemical composition are the fundamental concepts from which neurological functions develop.

The first approach to explain the neurobiological causes in bipolar disorder are through genes. Research has shown this disorder to be the one that is inheritable disorder. That means that if someone's family history includes a history that shows bipolar symptoms, it's most likely that the person will inherit the condition. If a person has grandparents or parents who were diagnosed with bipolar disorder, it is likely that they will be diagnosed with that mental illness.

The second method of studying neurological influences is neurotransmitters. Our brain is made up of chemicals that influence our mood, which is based on the quantity of the particular chemical. Dopamine, serotonin, and norepinephrine enter the picture. Any imbalance between the three hormones is likely to cause disturbance in the person's level of elation or depression. The changes in state result in an increase in manic moods and hypoactivity in depressive episodes.

Neuroimaging research has revealed that bipolar disorder may be associated with the part of the brain that is involved in emotions. There are significant shifts in activity that occur in the region that is involved in emotion. brain. These changes are in line with the degree of emotional reactivity that a person is. Research suggests how bipolar disorder can be connected to an increase in activity in the area of the brain that is involved in emotion as well as to an the increased the sensitivity of dopamine receptors that affect the state that the brain is in.

Apart from the biological factor which determines our body's makeup for susceptibility to bipolar disorder studies have shown that life events may cause bipolar disorder, especially those with depression episodes. Bipolar disorder is characterized by depression. is correlated with low support from social networks and low social capabilities. For instance, a person might be grieving the loss of an individual they love. Someone with weak social support and poor social skills is not likely to have a person to discuss the loss the individual is feeling and, as a result, will fall into depression.

Mania however is psychologically explained by important life events that lead to achievement of a goal. Reward-seeking behavior is closely dependent on the possibility of manic behaviors. It is believed that the success on a specific pursuit may causes changes in confidence that can increase the number of goals pursued. In addition to goal-setting sleep is also regarded as a contributor the bipolar condition. The disturbances to sleep and circadian rhythms may cause manic episodes. The research currently isn't certain of the cause that sleep deprivation could be the main cause of manic episodes. However, research has proven insomnia is a significant cause of bipolar disorder.

Chapter 10: A Depression that Doesn't Get Better

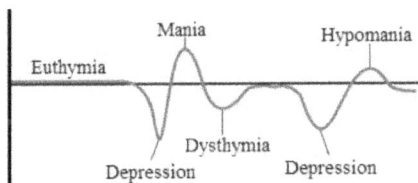

If there isn't any or little improvement, it is important to examine the cause of the failure of treatment. The most common causes of failure in treatment are:

The problem is often misdiagnosed.

Right diagnosis but incorrect medicine

Correct diagnosis and accurate medication but the wrong dosage

A proper diagnosis, drug and treatment, however, a poor period of time

If you are unsure of the diagnosis, treatment, or medication and the time frame you should look for the following causes:

Consistent use of substances:

Alcohol

Nicotine

Illegal drug use

The use of illicit drugs such as licent, narcotics

Drug interactions

Insufficient sleep and irregularity

The absence of psychotherapy

Inadequate diet

Physical exercise is not required.

No spiritual or religious activities

There is no family support

Social support is not available.

No or only partial reintegration into the academic and professional world

Take note! There isn't always what appears.

We should be aware that the term "depression" can have different meanings. It can refer to an illness, a syndrome or even a condition. It is important to know this in the selection of the best treatment.

Depression can be used as a synonym to mean sadness. Sadness is a typical and normal symptom that can be found in various life circumstances. It is a result of physical, psychological, or emotional stress. It generally doesn't require medical treatment (2).

The term depression is used to refer to a condition. A syndrome is a collection of symptoms and signs of an illness. In addition to sadness, it encompasses diverse other disorders, such as appetite, sleep as well as weight, sexual disorder and so on. It is similar to MDD in all ways, however it isn't MDD. The distinction is that the underlying cause of the condition is a mental or mental health illness different from MDD. Thus, treatment should be focused the disorder which "mimics" the symptoms of depression.

Hypothyroid patients may be prone to drowsiness and appetite increase as well as weight gain, sadness and fatigue and difficulty in concentrating, memory issues and many more like MDD. In such cases treatment is centered on replacing thyroid hormones. It is important to note that although the symptoms are identical to depression signs can be attributed to a common medical reason.

Other medical conditions can be associated with depression syndrome as the sole clinical manifestation. Even if there are just symptoms of emotional distress the patient should be assessed with care. We must exclude general medical issues because the treatment options are different.

The common medical ailments that are similar to depression and need extra caution include:

Thyroid Disease

Parathyroid Diseases

Anemia

Hypoxia (lack of oxygen)

Neoplasms (cancers)

The following diseases are caused by drugs:

Beta Blockers (drugs that are used to regulate blood pressure)

Calcium Channel Blockers (drugs used to manage blood pressure)

Steroids

Sedatives

Hormones

Central Nervous System (CNS) Disorders:

Dementia

Parkinson's Disease

Other CNS Disorders:

Huntington's Korea

Multiple Sclerosis

Ailments to the Frontal Lobe

Stroke

HIV Infections (AIDS)

Cushing's Syndrome

Treatment using corticosteroids

Systemic Lupus Erythematosus (SLE)

Other rheumatic disorders

If someone suffers the loss of a loved one could suffer from "depression" because it is a sign in the feeling of sadness. It could also be referred to as a disorder that includes various other symptoms of depression as well as grieving. In addition, the diagnosis of psychiatric illness could be that caused by depression that was caused by loss but not necessarily caused by it.

A psychiatrist or doctor is qualified to assess if there are any other mental or medical condition that is similar to depression. This is vital for diagnosis and prevention of the tragic outcomes. One of them is death due a serious medical issues.

The person could be suffering from depressive disorder as a result of an underlying brain tumor. If the person isn't properly examined, the tumor could not be identified and the person will receive treatment for depression, and then suffer the consequences of the tumor that is not treated. Exams of the mind and body including laboratory tests, imaging and imaging, if required can help rule out the possibility of depression-related medical conditions.

The mental illness diagnosis is a diagnosis of exclusion. This means that the diagnosis is only made after the other medical causes that aren't psychiatric are eliminated. We must also look into other mental disorders because they could manifest as "depression" as an underlying symptom, syndrome or as an independent illness.

If the issue is a mental illness that is similar to depression, treatment is targeted at that disorder. The patient might be "depressed" because he displays signs of schizophrenia (hallucinations as well as delusions). In this instance we will treat the patient with antipsychotics, but not antidepressants. A variety of psychiatric issues can exhibit depression-related symptoms. They include bipolar mood disorders and anxiety disorders, as well as personality disorders, dissociative disorders and many more.

The most common mental health disorders that are misinterpreted as MDD and that require different treatment options include:

Bipolar Mood Disorder - Mood Stabilizers

Dementias - Depends upon the signs and anticholinesterases

Anxiety Disorders: Antidepressants and cognitive and Behavior Treatment (CBT)

Substance use disorders (Alcohol and drugs) Treatment with support Psychotherapy

Psychosis - Antipsychotics

The presence of multiple medical disorders or conditions is common to MDD. In this scenario depression is an individual diagnosis that must be treated accordingly in addition to the treatment offered for any other medical or psychiatric ailments.

It is difficult when it comes to diagnosing depression due to the various factors that need to be ruled out. The doctor, particularly psychiatrists, are accountable for this issue. Don't worry about it and don't be ashamed because you did not "diagnosing" MDD. Every person should be able to recognize the existence of this disease and seek help from a professional.

This alone can bring about a significant change to the lives of everyone.

You have taken the very first and foremost step which is to go through this book. According to the old saying, having a good knowledge is half the fight! This gesture removes us from discrimination, prejudice, or ignorance. These can be huge barriers to the assessment and therapy of depression. This act alone can save lives! What could be that is more rewarding? The famous quote, "Whoever saves one life will save the entire world." It's true, especially when it comes to helping someone suffering from depression. Your role is to understand and assist as much as you can for those suffering from MDD. You could save lives and the planet.

If you're depressed Your job is to follow the guidelines to heal. The use of medication and psychotherapy as directed will benefit you over the long term. Regularly exercising as well as sleeping and eating properly and taking care of your spiritual or religious aspects, you can enhance the overall well-being of your family.

Bipolar mood disorder (BD) can be described as the most serious disorder that needs to recognize. Depression symptoms and signs are quite similar. What is different is the frequency of episodes of irritability and mood elevation (called the mania). Find out below how mood swings manifest in people suffering from BD (Figure 2.).

Figure 2. The blue line is a representation of the mood of the individual. We can see an average state (Euthymia) which is depicted by the horizontal black line. Under the lines, we are experiencing an unmotivated mood (Dysthymia) as well as depression (Depression). Over the top, we show an increase in levels of energy, activity (Hypomania) as well as more strongly increased the mood (Mania).

The treatment for depression in its pure form is accomplished by using antidepressants. Treatment for Bipolar Disorder is by mood stabilizers. Antidepressants used in bipolar disorder may cause manic episodes or may cause depression to worsen! If there's another mental illness that is similar to or is related to MDD The psychiatrist is the educated and accountable professional to choose the method of treatment.

Chapter 11: Scheduling and Prepare For Appointments

For you to start dealing with bipolar disorders, it is necessary to find a doctor , or an expert in mental health who can aid you. When choosing a doctor it is vital to choose a specialist in dealing with these types of disorders. For instance, you must pick a trusted and skilled psychiatrist who has experience in dealing with the cases of bipolar disorder.

As appointments aren't all that long, and there are many aspects that must be taken care of, you need to be ready. Therefore, prior to scheduling an appointment, ensure you're prepared and know what you can anticipate. Becoming prepared ahead of time will save you time , and also assures you the most benefit from the appointment.

What are the things You Must Do Prior to your appointment time?

Before your scheduled appointment It is vital to follow these steps to make sure that you don't lose any important information you wish to discuss or share about.

In the first place, you must record the symptoms and signs that you're experiencing. Even if there are some details you believe may not have anything to do with the appointment, it's a good idea to write them down. Patients are prone to lose these information, particularly when they're not recorded. This information set will aid the doctor assess the condition of your body.

Record your personal details as well as your current circumstances. As an example, you need to include any important information, such as recent developments within your personal life. If you're currently suffering from extreme stress, you must include these issues. Include any information or details you believe could be useful. Any change or experience that you experience in your daily life may have an consequences and could make your condition worse. These facts can aid your doctor treat your condition.

Write down all medications or supplements you're taking. If you're taking any medication, or are taking any vitamins or supplements it is crucial for you to note the details down. Even if they're just supplements, they can cause adverse effects if taken in conjunction with your prescription medication. Therefore, you must be cautious.

Make a list of questions you'd like for your doctor. It can also help if could bring along any close family members or friends. If you're feeling uneasy and have a difficult time as this is the first time you've talked to a medical professional about the condition you are experiencing, it's helpful when you have someone near you. As you become accustomed to the sessions and treatments you'll feel more at ease.

Things You Should Discuss to your doctor

Because your appointment isn't long it is important to think of the questions you would like to ask. Understanding the definition of bipolar disorder as well as other details you need to learn about your condition is essential. This will help you be aware of the factors that can aggravate your condition. Here are some items you could be able to ask your doctorabout:

Do I suffer with bipolar disorder?

What could be the reasons?

What triggers?

Are there any tests I must pass?

What are the treatments available and which is the most effective option to consider?

Are there potential negative side effects associated with one treatment?

Are there other options to treat bipolar disorder?

Could you suggest to me some books I could go through or a website that you could suggest?

What are the most important things I should do to minimize the aggravation of my health condition?

Is bipolar disorder curable?

What to Expect

When you visit the doctor or practitioner you choose You can anticipate to be asked questions. In order to help you determine the most effective treatment or cure alternative, ensure that you do not conceal any information, and simply be honest with your physician. Prepare yourself to answer them to aid your doctor in assessing your health. Your doctor might ask you the questions below:

Have you ever experienced the following symptoms and signs?

Do you often feel that you are experiencing mood swings or mood changes?

What are the signs and symptoms impact your day-to-day routine?

Do you know relatives of yours who suffer from bipolar disorder?

Are you experiencing suicidal thoughts or inclined to commit suicide?

Do you take drugs, consume alcohol, and smoke cigarettes?

Are you having issues or sleep issues?

Chapter 12: How Does It Feel Like to be a victim of Borderline Persuasion Disorder?

Although it's a great feeling at first to have this kind of break however, if it continues for over a long period, it can be like the suffering. It's obvious that you're experiencing something, but you aren't able to get yourself to worry about anything.

One time I was admitted to the hospital (yes it was a in the psych Ward) and the alarm for fire was activated. I didn't get up from my mattress. I was completely uninterested whether there was a fire. I was not worried.

I can remember feeling a little angry and thinking that, should there be an fire, then either somebody would be able to come and grab me or I'd end up dying. It didn't matter.

I also lose the ability to be concerned about others. When I'm talking to someone I know and she's angry and crying over her mother's death, died, I'm unable to be bothered to think about it.

Of sure, I'll cover my tracks and pretend to do and even make the right statements however it can be very exhausting. I'll get annoyed being with someone who's physically hurt and won't be quiet.

I'm aware that this is wrong But I just can't stop this. If I am feeling emotions I'm extremely caring and compassionate. The contrast between these two states is astounding.

There are also constant feelings of emptiness and boredom. They can cause a person to engage in dangerous behaviors, such as:

Abuse of alcohol and drugs

Shopping sprees, or spending money

Driving recklessly and speeding

Purging and bingeing (eating disorders are fairly typical in borderlines, regardless of whether it's BED Bulimia, BED, or Anorexia)

Sexual promiscuity

Self-mutilation (usually cutting oneself)

A person suffering from BPD may not show the risky behaviors listed above however self-mutilation is thought to be a sign for the condition.

The person feels overwhelmed by negative emotions and desperately attempts to escape by making physical pain, so they don't feel emotional discomfort for a while.

Sometimes, they cut as they are disengaged from reality. They don't feel authentic and everything around them doesn't seem real.

It's a bit disturbing. When they cut themselves and see blood flowing and the blood flowing, it assures them that they're real.

Sometimes cutting doesn't like the physical pain however, watching their own blood can be very satisfying and relaxing. It can really help calm the person. It is a strange feeling to watch the flow of your own blood is as the effects of a drug.

This brings us to a different reason that cutting, particularly severe, can trigger an intense surge of endorphins. This is the reason cutting can be addicting as a drug.

Another characteristic of Borderline is that Borderline one of the characteristics is they possess a highly scattered sense of their identity. There are times when I don't have any concept of who I are or what I would like to be.

This is another reason that many Borderlines are extremely talented actors. We are able to alter who we are in response to the circumstance. We continually try various identities.

I'm a different person based on the person I am with at the moment. It's not a conscious choice I simply switch identities without being conscious of it.

I'm not the same person when I'm with my family members than with my colleagues or my partner. In addition, I'm different depending on the person I'm with right now.

This is the reason I've observed that the majority of Borderlines tend to their friends to keep their lives separate. I usually prefer spending time with my friends in a private setting.

It can be a bit confusing to determine the person you're with in when you're in a crowd but this is precisely why acting skills are so beneficial.

Borderlines generally have a sharp sense of smell and are able to "read" the other person extremely well. It also helps with empathy because we can detect how others are feeling.

There is always the fear of losing their loved ones. This could make certain Borderlines to be insecure and dependent, which naturally, is typically quite off-putting to people around them.

The worst they can be is their personal enemies because the thing they fear most is being abandoned and often they result in driving people away because of it.

Others aren't needy and may appear cold at times without realizing that. Personally, I do not have any particular person in my life.

It doesn't mean that I don't like people, however. However, if someone doesn't wish to be my friend I won't keep them to be there.

Borderlines are well-known for their turbulent relations with family, friends and loved ones. Sometimes they are angry due to an apparent rejection or denial.

There is nobody who is more passionately in love than someone with BPD. They're also among the most loyal and trustworthy companions you could have, and they are likely to stay with regardless of the situation.

Unless you commit a crime against them.

There is no person who could be hated more intensely than Borderline. The intensity of his rage and anger is awe-inspiring to others.

People who suffer from BPD typically view the world in stark dark and black. Some are highly valued or are incredibly hated.

I personally don't know many people I am neutral with.

It's the same for our beliefs about morality and goodness. There is often a fierce internal conflict within us over whether we'd like the best or evil.

We believe in being true to our word when we make it clear to someone, and do not compromise a trust.

Depression is a common occurrence within Borderlines. It is common for mood swings to range from deep of despair, to feelings of almost euphoria can be a regular circumstance.

This is one reason that most Borderlines are often misinterpreted as bipolar. However, they can be concomitant.

Antidepressants can be beneficial however they do not appear to be as effective on someone suffering from BPD like they do for those who suffer from depression only.

Are the symptoms of Borderline Personality Disorder worse than having Bipolar Disorder?

In cases of extreme display it's nearly impossible for a person to respond. being unable to lead a like a normal person with human relations that are normal is a devastating experience regardless of the reason; and debating over which is the worst is like debating the best method of dying. The truth is that when you're done with each experience the result is a smack of rocks.

When we are talking about presentations that are less extreme the situation gets more complicated. Personality Disorders aren't as responsive to medication as BPD is. However, people who recognize they suffer from such conditions and are looking to reduce their effects have a greater chance of limiting the effects of their condition by hard work, perseverance and determinationby focusing their attention on self-awareness, behavioral techniques and meta-cognition. They also attend appropriate therapy for their behavior and more.

In the meantime, a person suffering from BPD may benefit benefits from all these methods however due to the character of the disorder can literally affect the psychological strength required to make it through the day or reducing it to the point that just functioning is an actual battle (in depression cycles) or raising it to the point of being that the patient feels unlimited in their abilities. Thus, non-pharmacological treatments have beneficial however, they often have less effects.

For the personality Disorder sufferer, the positive side is that they don't need to endure the many adverse side effects that come with medication. The downside is because very few drugs are more effective than placebo effects on patients suffering from personality disorders. Patients may experience some relief from many medications, but ultimately they aren't efficient, if you look at them in terms of.

BPD sufferers, however, have a lot to gain from medications up to the point that even those with very severe symptoms are able to live normal lives. However, this comes at a price of having to endure numerous unpleasant negative side effects. The biggest challenge to BPD treatments is often the continued conformity. BPD sufferers are more likely to stop taking their medications.

The disorders are very distinct in their responses to treatment and the best treatment impacts on the individual as well as negative. Which"is "worse," from a standpoint of clinical practice is about which set of consequences the individual patient will take the most. Since you aren't able to randomly assign mental illness to patients to determine how they react this isn't something to be resolved in an manner that is objective.

From the perspective of therapists from a psychiatrist's perspective: the majority of psychiatrists. If asked, they would say they're much more willing to deal with patients with BPD patient rather than the person with a personality disorder due to the fact that patients are more likely to react well to the appropriate medications. The psychiatrist also has plenty of instruments to aid the patient and be more confident in their ability to achieve a positive outcome for the patient. However, the majority of psychologists and therapists who specialize in behavioral therapies such as CBT and DBT will likely be more willing to help a person suffering from an emotional disorder for the same reason. Their top tools offer them greater chances of being capable of helping.

Can borderline personality disorders be treated?

I've read that borderlines improve if you maintain them until they turn 35. At that point, they're supposed to be settled in a certain family and identity, and career path that helps will stabilize and organize their lives.

(Whoever wrote that was not thinking about the seven years that followed the recession)

LOL

They weren't even thinking about other things.

Judy Garland is said to be a borderline, and her life was worse and worse getting worse.

Here's my experience.

As a teenager, I was filled with dreams and fantasies of who I would to be and what my life would be like. For me, the concept of wholeness was built around the idea of transformation. The idea that all my primary BPD issues would disappear. Then I'd become an entirely new person with an entirely new life.

I am a hugely rooted on the world of creativity and have devoted a lot of my life to making characters in plays and performing various characters in the theatre and in films. This is why I believed that I would transform into a person who did not have any of these issues.

Maria Callas was one who believed in the ugly duckling swan story. Get rid of the fat, abused girl and transform into a beautiful and a diva. Becoming. This was the story about her existence. "Everything is ....a changing into". -Maria Callas.

Therefore, I was totally disconnected and disconnected from the person I was at the base. My core wasn't part the process. I believed that I would become somebody other than myself. For decades.

As Bradshaw once stated. "I lived in the middle of my driveway, and my home was burning."

A quick and easy thing to throw into the mix. One thing that really defined my life in my teenage years were my narcissistic characteristics. I was very involved in creating a wonderful life, having amazing friendships and a stunning persona. an incredible identity. Within the framework there was no room for emotional reactivity. It was also a problem of identity, suicide or inability to self control my emotions. (The BPD Dance). I wasn't having it. I wasn't having all of that. I was required to act in order in order to live the life I wanted and become my ideal self be. That's the way I went about it. Victory on the part of our will. Over trauma and emotion, and the past and the present. It's dangerous to base your performance on willpower:

What happened? Why did things become worse with time? Because I'm sure you've already knew that's why I'm going to say to you...

As I grew older, all the shiny, sparkly things my narcissistic youth craved, ended up being too low-quality. Then they were no longer able to make me behave in order to get them.

It's like the emotionally troubled kids in a group home actually are able to get together in a token economy. They are capable of keeping all their problems at bay while striving to rise up the economic ladder and gain all the benefits. It's the same with Will power.

Once you've exhausted yourself of the perks , everything goes into hell. The will flags begin to fly.

This is exactly what happened to me.

What did my concept of becoming a person? So, I was one, created an identity as that person, and I gradually got very comfortable being the new person and becoming this person was real to me , and wasn't filling me with imagination and fantasy no longer, and as disassociation disintegrated the majority of my issues began to arise. Being real was extremely dangerous for me. The result was that I became a person living a different life. Then another. Utilizing different aspects of me for each reinvention , and segregating from other parts of me, my history, and my memories left and right.

At the age of 44 I was an absolute glamourous train wreck waiting to take place.

Someone was just waiting to make a move!

(Opps. Mixed metaphor)

It was for me that light match and the Train crash happened because at 45, I experienced an enormous blow-up with my family members when I suffered a health problem during the downturn , which triggered every single safety concern I've ever had from the deep, deep, and deep to the bottom. The way that my family let me down and abandoned me in the midst of this crisis was a slap to me!

This also happened because I was the person I hoped to be and each one of them brought me closer to the separation I required to be able to endure because success in becoming meant that I was entering into reality. If you are able to become the person you want to be, you are no longer able to feel the disconnecting from the dream that it gives you. You are pulled out of the opium pit of the imagination.

When I was 50, I discovered myself being dragged by the passage of time, life and circumstances into the heart of my issues. I'd been using my fantasies and imagination, as well as alcohol , spending as well as drugs, people, things and places to stay out of this situation when I was just 2 1/2 years old.

And now ....There Was I!

I'm going through what Masterson refers to as the depression of abandonment that took eight years to resolve and left me lying to my back in bed depressed and in need of medication, as well as in a state of disability.

So no. Borderline personality disorder didn't improve for me over time. The exact opposite happened. It turned into a complete fucking nightmare.

The positive news, because it's not over until when the fat girl sings. (Someone ought to have told that to Maria Callas). At this point, I was totally dragged into my boiling core which was depression being the sole factor that was keeping me in a stable state. A complete shut-down and becoming a total zombie kept me from getting into the abysmal state of chaos, crisis and frustration, anger and despair and anxiety and fear that is the very core of borderline.

Depression, a crippling depression, is a expensive cost to pay to maintain homeostasis. A life of paralysis and dying in the end is not the best option.

Through some miraculous process, the depression began to ease gradually. Because there was a lot of me who wanted to be free of it and there were so many internal resources waiting to be gathered by me. them and bring them together. Utilize them to be healed.

So on one hand, I am reconnecting with my Inner resources, and on my other side I have to deal with my borderline emotional conglomeration to the very first time I have ever dealt with it. This has lowered my performance.

However, I'd rather die than try to block it all out using medications. I would really like to get through it.

The emotional depths of my being in the end, I was able to behave badly within my personal relationships. I was slamming my family. Becoming a bit snarky with my friends. My narcissistic tendencies which kept me in a state of disarray and snoozing are gone.

I'm really in need of tackle all the symptoms of being borderline as well as do the emotional healing that is the core of my work.

Making great progress. Finally. Since I'm finally expressing my true self and where I'm at. It was impossible to believe that I could ever heal without this. Unfortunately, every thing I've ever had in my life was utilized to escape from the area .

That's why I wasn't getting better and better and better, and then settle in a state of mind at the age of 35. This is the reason I was a mess and dissociated and depressed, stressed and in crisis, and hoping to die at 50.

Today, at 58, I'm sure I'm going up and up, and there's a chance.

In the end, I chose to take the long route.

What is the definition of Borderline personality disorder (emotionally unstable personality disorder) refer to? What are the symptoms?

Depression, with extreme sadness, or violent or angry behaviour to hide this sadness

Self-esteem is low, and they generally believe that they are the worst of themselves. In some instances there are moments when they feel proud of themselves, however this is to help combat the depression however, they eventually be back to the same state.

Many mood swings that occur on a regular basis or the same day

Insane behavior is a result of a lack of instruction from their parents how to handle the intense emotions and frustrations when they were children, so they reverberate through their behavior

They are inclined to either admire people, imagining them to be perfect, or they could be able to see the same person the next moment as a monster who is responsible for all the mistakes they've made in their lives, generally there's no room for middle ground as you're either perceived as the greatest or the most awful

An overwhelming fear of being abandoned and clinging to you however, if you're close to them, they may disengage due to their fear of intimacy, because they fear they will be exposed to the public how pathetic and unworthy they that they are. It's like Hedgehogs that seek one another to warm themselves, but they poke each other due to their spikes

Do you have instances of verbal or physical violence

They are a way for people to fulfill themselves, and without them, people feel unsatisfying. They also have a positive nature. They can't be able to bear the absence of another person, whether real or imagined, as it can trigger feeling of guilt and abandonment, which is unbearable to their loved ones. They also require a continuous source of love and attention by the person within the relationship. In the relationship, each person should be considered to be a part of them and not as an distinct individual, resulting in dependent relationships.

They may be manipulative emotionally

Self-destructive behavior, such as self-harming, and all activities that hurt them at the end and then feel a massive amount of guilt later due to the fact that they believed they caused their own lives and the lives of others in a mess. This guilt isn't a result of an incident but rather an ongoing feeling that they are unnaturally bad.

They are unable to endure void inside their chests

They are very confused about their identity and are suffering from identity issues.

They may be susceptible to addictive tendencies.

They are struggling with relationships

Sexual inhibition or promiscuity

I don't know whether I have covered all the bases However, these signs or signs may or may not show up in people with The Borderline Personality Disorder There are many different people with the disorder and thus exhibit different signs and not show all of them. This is also due to the different levels in the condition. They suffer from many times in their lives. They think they're ruining their lives and those who surround them. They want to be accepted by others and that people can see that they aren't really doing their actions.

Chapter 13: Treatment Borderline Personality Disorder

The diagnosis could be surprising, disappointing or a cause for concern for a person with BPD. It can be a source of shock, disappointment, or even annoy. However, BPD responds well to treatment, regardless of the effect it has on an individual's life. People who are suffering should anticipate to experience a permanent improvement if they step out of the shadows and seek treatment. Psychotherapy, typically supported by a mix of drugs, skills education and holistic healing methods to restore health and vitality as the mainstay of BPD treatment strategies.

Making a diagnosis

The borderline personality disorder (BPD) diagnosis is difficult for those working in the field in the field of mental health. The symptoms of BPD are often in conjunction with other mental illnesses and its frequency is often under-estimated and usually occurs when there are similar or contradicting symptoms that could make it difficult to determine the diagnosis.

But, once a clear diagnosis of BPD is made the chances are high for healing. BPD patients seeking professional assistance will be able to access to a track record of success with special therapies as well as other treatment techniques.

BPD Treatment Program

As long as treatment is not initiated for the disorder borderline personality, the medical professional is assigned to oversee and coordinate the entire patient rehabilitation program. Goals or objectives are set to motivate the patient to assure a steady recovery rate. Programs for healing are modified to incorporate new methods or strategies in cases where there is or have not been any advancements.

While individuals differ however, the general structure of the BPD recovery plan typically includes the following fundamental characteristics:

* In-person, group and psychotherapy for families. Treatment centered on drugs is now the norm for various kinds of mental illnesses, with the help of therapy. However, the situation is different when it comes to BPD. Therapy remains the primary component for all BPD treatment plans. And specific therapeutic strategies for dealing with the unique symptoms of this extremely common disease have been developed.

* Medication. There aren't any medications specifically designed to treat BPD. However, prescription medications are still in use to improve the symptoms or conditions of BPD.

Life skills learning and training. Sessions in the classroom that offer patients information about the specifics associated with their health issues and teach them how to manage symptoms and issues in their lives have become the norm in the administration of mental health regimens.

Healing through holistic methods. Alongside more traditional methods of therapy The holistic mind-body approach is beneficial to those suffering from BPD because of two reasonsfirstly, they can help reduce stress, and in addition, they aid people in developing more control and self-control.

Additional treatment services are available for health conditions that co-occur. If other mental health disorders or addiction issues are discovered the treatment programs should treat these disorders simultaneously while paying the focus on BPD symptoms.

People who suffer from a borderline suicidal personality disorder could have to be admitted in psychiatric facilities until the situation is resolved or experience severe instances of symptoms dissociative.

Different kinds of Therapy for Bipolar Personality Disorder (BPD)

Psychotherapy is an integral part of the borderline personality disorder healthcare program that is offered to outpatients and inpatients. The majority of the men and women who seek BPD care will receive individual or family counseling. Sessions are scheduled when needed.

Although each is unique there is a minimum of two psychotherapy types are included in the most well-known treatment strategies:

Dialectic Behavioural Therapy (DBT)

As the gold standard for BPD treatment, DBT was mainly designed to treat the condition. The therapy helps develop techniques for managing stress and emotional regulation self-confidence, attention and interpersonal communication , with practical guidelines that focus on health overall and the health and quality of life.

MBT -Mentalization-Based Therapy (MBT)

The therapy based on mentalization is designed to improve the capacity for BPD sufferers to understand their behavior and feelings in relation to certain mental states, not only on their own, but also with others. Another method of treatment is developed specifically for BPD sufferers. Once they have this information patients will begin to comprehend their condition as a precursor towards their recovery.

CBT is a form of cognitive therapy. (CBT)

Cognitive-behavioral therapy is an important element of many treatment methods for mental health issues, including ones that offer assistance to patients suffering from this condition. Through CBT sessions patients are taught to change negative thinking patterns into more constructive and positive thoughts until the behaviors are established.

Eye-Movement Desensitization as well as Reprocessing (EMDR)

By combining physical exercise and the ability to focus on the mind, EMDR therapy helps patients suffering from mental illness to deal with previous traumas without fear and in a space that is solely focused on recovery and health.

-Transference-Focused-Psychotherapy (TFP)

In this case, the primary concentration is on establishing the positive, supportive relation between patient and therapy provider, and then acting as an ideal model to guide the patient's behavior and psychological rehabilitation.

-Schema-Focused-Psychotherapy (SFT)

The primary method of psychotherapy assists patients to deal with their difficulties through alternating between five types or regimens which define the BPD person's personality (according according to SFT theory) which include: confused and abandoned children, angry and impulsive kids as well as the unconditional protector the punitive parent as well as healthy adult.

-Systems-Training-For-Emotional-Predictability and Problem-Solving (STEPPS)

This is a 20-week , outpatient group therapy program that combines cognitive-behavioral retraining and practical skills. The sessions of training include family members as well as friends to assist BPD sufferers build a solid support network and caregivers.

-Family Psycho-education

The therapy is designed to provide family members of BPD patients with advice with information, guidance, and emotional support for their benefit and ensures their complete participation in the treatment program.

Additional Therapies for Co-Occurring Disorders

If co-occurring disorders are identified and treatment is required, it's also important. Integrated behavioral or mental health programs are created specifically to manage multiple disorders at once as well as the vast majority of treatments in a typical BPD treatments program could be modified to address other mental health issues.

BPD MEDICATIONS

There aren't any drugs specially designed to treat BPD are available for treatment. Two classes of drugs are nevertheless, effective in fighting the most debilitating BPD symptoms including mood stabilizers as well as anti-psychotics.

Anti-psychotics: They are generally prescribed for schizophrenia. However, when they are administered in smaller doses, the severity of the perceptual and cognitive distortions that BPD sufferers typically suffer from can be diminished. Paranoia, extreme thoughts, and dissociative events can significantly affect women and men however, anti-psychotics can aid in managing the symptoms and help them reconnect with reality.

Mood stabilizers They are the treatment that are recommended for BPD patients who battle emotional vulnerability and impulsivity. They may help reduce the severity of BPD aggressive anger sufferers and help to combat the crippling anxiety that is often associated with this mental health condition that is all-encompassing.

Skills Training as well as the Holistic Healing Process and education

The majority of BPD sufferers benefit from advanced education programs that help them learn strategies for dealing with the symptoms of BPD. Self-management skills are crucial to ensure the safety and wellbeing of those suffering from mental health issues, as the drugs are not always effective and therapists may not be always available outside of the treatment center.

While waiting classes in information can help people with restricted personality disorders gain understanding of their condition and help them understand the underlying issues that could hinder them from committing to recovery. The knowledge gained from the classes regarding BPD will help those in the beginning stages to identify symptoms and give them more of an understanding of where they are in the spectrum of borderline personality disorders.

In mental health facilities that are residential holistic methods for healing the mind and body are available in the present and could be beneficial to people suffering from BPD in the ambulatory program. BPD sufferers have issues managing their emotions and holistic methods are developed to address this specific issue.

Below are a few of the effective methods for healing the body and mind for those suffering from mental health disorders:

* Acupuncture

* Yoga

* Meditation

* Music Therapy or Art

* Therapy with horses

* Tai Chi

* Massage therapy

* Dietary therapy

The holistic treatment methods are a great way to boost the health of those who suffer from BPD and not just from illnesses, since they help to re-energize their bodies, minds and bodies.

Hospitalization for treatment of BPD. Disorder (BPD)

In clinics, 10 % of patients receiving outpatient treatment and as high as 20 percent of patients are receiving residential care. These figures are astonishing because they show the understanding of mental health professionals that residential treatment facilities are crucial in the first stages of rehabilitation for BPD patients.

If individuals with a mild personality disorder are dedicated and dedicated to seeking outpatient treatment and rehabilitation, they have an opportunity to attain an extended period of symptom-free health. However, to guarantee the best outcomes, it's best to begin treatment is to go to an inpatient treatment center for the majority of BPD patients. What you learn during your the stay-in-care program will be with you when you are back in your normal life and will also provide you with an excellent foundation to build on when you transition to the less demanding ambulatory treatment program.

The general consensus is that the path to recovery after diagnosis is great for women and men suffering from BPD and demonstrates how the medical field has profited from this historically poorly understood disorder.

Utilizing COGNITIVE BEHAVIORAL Therapy to treat BPD

CBT is a kind of psychotherapy that can be utilized to treat depression. CBT is a form of psychotherapy.

A one-on-one session with a therapist may be a requirement for psychotherapy. It may also require groups sessions between the psychotherapist as well as other patients with similar issues.

Although different approaches are employed but they all assist patients regulate their thoughts, emotions and behaviours. Psychotherapy can also be a venue where patients can find positive answers to issues.

What is the best way to incorporate CBT Integrate into Your Treatment?

Typically, a mix of psychotherapy and medicine is the most effective treatment of bipolar disorders. CBT is among the most popular psychotherapy types.

CBT is a tool that can be utilized in a variety of ways. it includes:

* Handling the mental health issues

* Avoidance of behaviours that may result in a return of these symptoms.

• Learning effective strategies for coping to ease feelings and anxiety

* Used as an alternative treatment when medications fail or aren't an option.

What is the CBT method of treatment?

The primary goal the main goal of CBT is to assist you to gain a new view of your current situation. CBT accomplishes this by challenging the negative beliefs and fears in a clear manner and assisting you in overcoming or get rid of the negative thoughts and fears.

Most often, treatment is short-term and focuses on the reduction or the treatment of particular problems. This is inclusive of your as well as the therapist's.

The therapist and you must be working together on the following topics during the CBT session:

Find out the cause of mental health, stress, job or any other issue that could be causing you anxiety.

Review the behavior, emotions and thoughts related to BPD

After you've established the issue, you are able to begin working with the counselor to determine what you do to address them.

Find out if you have negative or unclear emotions, actions, or feelings.

There are many ways to look at or deal with issues that make the situation more difficult. This could include thinking negative about your own situation or dwelling on the negative aspects of a situation or situation.

Make a change in your attitude towards personal issues.

The therapist and the client collaborate to replace negative thoughts by more positive and constructive ones in sessions. This could include a positive outlook on your capacity to handle the situation as well as a more objective understanding of the circumstances.

Who can take CBT?

The use of cognitive-behavioral therapy in the majority of instances can be effective. In several locations, such as the private and hospital settings, psychotherapy may be provided. It is among the most popular forms of therapy. Many employers provide psychotherapy through their support programs for employees.

What are the adverse effects?

Psychotherapy is not a cause of physical consequences. If you choose to go through CBT you can freely speak to a therapist or even an entire group of people regarding your issues. It can be a frustrating experience and challenging to overcome.

CBT is a popular treatment that addresses a range of disorders such as managing bipolar disorder. The purpose of this therapy is to understand the causes and reactions to these concerns and responses. It will then determine which reactions are harmful and substitutes the ones that are toxic with healthier alternatives.

Chapter 14: What Can You Do to Improve Social Relations

There aren't many rules to aid you in making an impression. Take a look at the five points laid below and you'll have an possibility to interact with an array of members of a social network.

Lights for the start

When they first meet or getting more familiar with someone, there are many people who will bombard the other person with a series of "talk with fashion" questions. (Where are you from? What are you doing? What would you like from to do it? And the list goes further.). The kind of conversation isn't just exhausting; it's incredibly awkward to reply to an avalanche of questions from someone about whom you don't have the slightest clue about.

Instead of kicking out the door open with these types of questions If you're in the ideal scenario to start this show on the road by delivering a few informal, non-content talk. You can, for instance comment on something that's you observe in your surroundings. You could also you can open up by a bit of playful poking (simply be sure to keep smiling whenever you make a fuss to let her know that you're not joking). If you're not enjoying the conversation, you could usually begin by giving praise - perhaps for something they're wearing that you like.

Assemble affinity

In every social gathering, no matter whether it's a business meeting or having a drink with a lady in an establishment, it's essential to establish a strong bond. What can you do to achieve this? It is possible to start by using the "I" view in your discussions about your thoughts, feelings and conclusion. As an example instead of telling people that "b-ball is the most enjoyable game ever" as if it's a goal-oriented thing, you could say "I am a huge fan of B-ball" and maybe talk about the benefits you learn from it and why you enjoy it.

It might appear as an unnoticeable contrast, but using this "I" viewpoint lets people see your inner world, your thoughts, emotions and more. Furthermore is that when you show people this more enlightened look, they can see that you are someone who has a similar experience to them. This creates a strong bond that makes people feel more connected with you.

Provide services

A certain attitude can greatly assist you when you are in a social group. It is difficult to attain every now and then but it is possible that you're able to get people to wish to join with you however much it is anticipated. That is the view of a business.

When making connections, do not expect to "get" something. Don't contact a young woman trying to get a contact number, or to connect with a VIP business person to ensure that he'll exhibit improvements. If you're trying to build an established relationship with this young lady in order for her to be able to date you, or for that VIP wants to associate to a career begin by offering value first. Try to make the young lady a memorable meeting and brighten her day. Give the VIP the chance to overcome whatever problem that he might be facing. If you are constantly giving, without a intention of receiving anything in return many people will feel obliged to return the favor. This young lady is likely to provide you with her contact number and the VIP is expected to assist in obtaining an amazing career. It's not going to happen every time, but for the longest time, focusing on what you can provide instead of what you can receive will result in huge earnings.

Don't be ineffective

In almost every type of social connection, people are worried about what they get snubbed by. It's extremely uplifting when someone tells them that it's okay to take off the "social curtain". It means they no longer have to stress about how for "look nice" and look cool with their appearance, and be who they are and be acknowledged.

One of the best ways to make this entrance open and demonstrate to others that it's acceptable to relax, unwind and be yourself is to be the leader and leave yourself in the dust. For instance, if you're unsure regarding some aspect (your weight, the way you're dressed, how nervous you are...) Don't try to hide it, and hope that nobody takes note. Instead, shine a huge shine on the issue. It's ok to make fun of your own self for the fault (simply do not act as if you're naturally joking). Making a point of highlighting your flaws and laughing at them can make other people feel less stressed contemplating their flaws. To add a little additional, it is an amazing method of creating incredible connections.

Be positive and keep it that way

There isn't any kind of social interaction that can be altered by a negative frame of mind. The more positive and constructive you are in your interactions as well as your interactions with others, the more people will be happy to work with you. All things considered, the way you behave can be infective. Additionally in the event you need to remain friendly and positive in an interaction you will rub off your friends. Additionally, they'll appreciate being around you.

Effective Communication - Enhancing your Social Skills

Being able to build strong relationships with others can greatly reduce pressure and stress in your life. Actually, improving your social interaction is linked to better mental health overall, as having a great group of friends can serve as "support" for feelings of apathy and sour mood. But, as for some people, their anxiety can contribute to their inability to deal with social interactions, and hinder them from developing relationships. This is especially the case when you're feeling anxious and are frantically trying to find friends, but feel not able to consider making the effort or are unsure about how to interact with other people.

Unfortunately, one result of keeping the distance of a separation from the social world is that you don't have the opportunity to:

Build your confidence in interacting with other people.

Build strong interpersonal skills which will increase the chances to make connections that are effective

For example, on the off possibility that you're afraid of going to gatherings or inviting someone out for a night out the lack of knowledge as well as your lack of certainty can make it more difficult to determine how you will manage these situations (like the appropriate attire, how to present yourself etc.). Most of the time, people have the necessary skills, but aren't able to demonstrate the confidence to use these skills. Whatever the case, practicing can increase your confidence and enhance your interpersonal skills.

What are the reasons why communication Skills Essential?

These skills are essential to create (and maintaining) connections and to build an effective social community of individuals. They can also aid you in managing your personal requirements, while also being aware of the needs of other people. The majority of people are not brought to the world with exceptional interpersonal skills; as with other abilities, they are learned through trial and error and repeated practices.

Three different areas of correspondence you may need to practice are:

Non-verbal correspondence

Discussion aptitudes

Insistency

Note: Naturally there are many aspects to compelling correspondence, and you might need more explicit help in particular areas (for instance, figuring out how to handle conflict and introduction skills, giving critique, etc.). To get more specific assistance in cases where you're not having trouble, look up your "Prescribed readings" list towards the end of this course.

Non-Verbal Communication

The majority of the information we share with our fellow humans is non-verbal. The words you speak to others using your eyes or non-verbal communication can be just as impressive as what you communicate through words. If you are feeling anxious you might behave in ways that are designed to avoid speaking to other people. For instance, you could be cautious about eye-to-eye contact or speak with a soft tone. In the final analysis, you're doing what you can to transmit, but to avoid being thought to be a negative influence by others. In any event your non-verbal communication and style of speech sends incredible messages to other people about you:

State of passion (for example , eagerness or anxiety,)

A frame of mind toward the public (for instance, apathy, disdain)

Information about the topic

Realness (do do you possess a mysterious plan?)

As a result, in the event you are keeping a distance of eye-to-eye contact while avoiding other people and speaking in a discreet manner in a quiet manner, you're likely to be expressing, "Avoid me!" or "Don't engage me!" This isn't the message you want to convey.

Discussion Skills

Perhaps the most important test for someone with social tension is to start conversations and sustaining them. It's not unusual to be at war with one another when trying to have a conversation as it's not always simple to take into consideration remarks. This is evident especially when you are feeling anxious. On the other hand, some the edge keep on going and can cause an adverse effect on other people.

Self-assuredness

Self-assured communication is the authentic communication of one's desires, feelings and needs in relation to the individual's needs, feelings and desires. When you speak clearly your message, you are non-compromising and uncritical and you accept responsibility for your own actions.

If you're on edge socially it is possible that you will have difficulties communicating your thoughts and feelings in a clear manner. Self-assurance skills can be challenging to master, especially since being self-assured could result in avoiding the way you normally do things. In other words, you may be afraid of conflict, constantly be a good sport to the group and refrain from expressing your opinions. So, you could have developed an uninvolved style of correspondence. However you might be expecting to be able to dominate and control others and have developed an aggressive style of correspondence.

As it happens the use of an explicit correspondence style offers numerous benefits. It can, for instance, aid you in relating with people more effectively without fear and resentment. It also allows you to have more control over your life and reduces feelings of being in powerlessness. In addition, it gives other people to lead their lives.

Instructions for Behaving Assertively
Myths about assertiveness

The Fantasy 1: assertiveness CAN IMPLY getting your OWN way all the time

It's not true. Confidently sharing your viewpoint and discussing honestly with other people. In many cases, you don't be able to express "your unique style" when you're giving your opinion. However that you are expressing your feelings and trying to negotiate a deal off shows respect for you and others.

Legend #2: BEING ASSERTIVE MEANS BEING SELFISH

It's a flimsy claim. Since you are expressing your thoughts and desires doesn't mean that others have to comply with you. If you communicate what is required in a confident manner (not with force) then you have to account for others. It is also possible to be adamant to benefit an individual (for example , I could ask Susan to select the café next week).

Fantasy #3: PASSIVITY IS THE WAY TO BE LOVED

It's a flimsy. Uninvolved in your methods, you are constantly in agreement with other people, allowing them to live their lives in their way and allowing them to follow their own desires and not making any demands or requirements from your side. Doing this does not guarantee that people are going to like or appreciate you. The truth is people may view yourself as dull and confused that they are unable to get to know you better.

Fantasy #4: IT'S IMPOLITE TO DISAGREE

This isn't true. However, it is true that there are instances where we do not draw a logical conclusion (for instance, many people comment on how beautiful an individual looks in his wedding gown, or simply say positive things in the first day of taking a new job). The majority often, however the other people will be keen about what you believe. Consider how you'd be if everyone always agreed with your views.

Fantasy #5: I HAVE TO DO EVERYTHING I AM ASKED TO DO

Bogus. One of the most important aspects of being confident is defining and sustaining personal limits. This can be difficult for certain people. In the presence of our acquaintances we might insist that they believe we are arrogant and a bit smug when we don't answer all the questions they ask. When at work, we could be concerned that other employees will believe we're lazy or inefficient in the event that we do not complete the things we're asked to do. However, other people will never in any way in any way, or manner, realize how busy you are and how much you dislike an errand or the various plans you've made until you inform them. Many people be horrified to find out that you've done something for them but did not have the time for (for instance, preparing an essay that requires you to finish it by the at the end of each week) or something you really dislike doing (for instance, helping your friend relocate).

Chapter 15: What Risk Factors and Causes of Bipolar Disorder?

The precise reason for bipolar disorder is still to be unsolved. Researchers are still looking for the reasons that might be responsible for the disorder. Many believe that it is due to multiple causes that are interconnected to cause the disorder or circumstances that increase the risk. These causes include both environmental and genetic elements that are likely to play a role on a variety of levels, playing an important role in the development and onset that are associated with bipolar disorders.

Genetic influences

Bipolar disorder is usually caused by genetic. Recent statistics show that around half of people who suffer from bipolar disorder have an ancestral blood line (e.g. sibling, parent) with mental disorders like obsessive-compulsive disorders (OCD) or depression. This information prompted researchers to search for genes that may increase the risk for developing bipolar disorder. Genes act as helpers, they control the way that the human brain and body function. They form an fundamental to heredity and are that are encoded in the cells of an individual and are passed down from parents to children.

Statistics:

The results of studies show that a child with a parent who suffers from bipolar disorder is likely to have a 15 to 25 percent chance of experiencing the same mental issue.

A person who has an identical twin diagnosed with this condition has an opportunity of 25% of having the same illness.

Someone with an identical twin suffering from bipolar disorder is at an even higher chance to develop the exact disorder since identical twins have the exact same genetic material. This increases the risk by around eight times the risk compared to twins who are not identical.

Environmental factors

In addition to genetic causes Researchers believe that additional risk factors could increase the likelihood of developing bipolar disorder. Recent studies of identical twins have demonstrated that not every twins of people who suffers from this disorder suffer from bipolar disorder. This suggests that different factors, other than genes, are in play. This could now be the environmental. Certain characteristics were noted, including:

Abuse of alcohol and drugs, bad habits and even hormonal disorders can induce depressive or manic symptoms even for those with no the family history of bipolar disorder.

Events in life like trauma, stress, abuse or the death of a loved ones trigger extreme mood swings in those who has a family background for bipolar disorders.

The first signs of bipolar disorder begin to manifest at a young the age of. This is believed to be the result of various social and environmental elements that are still to be fully understood.

Substance abuse is a major factor in the development of bipolar disorder throughout the time of recovery. Alcohol and tranquilizers may cause extreme depression.

Neurochemical factors

The imbalance in certain brain chemicals called neurotransmitters is believed to play a major part in the development of mood disorders, especially those with bipolar. Neurotransmitters are chemical messengers that include serotonin and norepinephrine among others that are responsible for this disorder. Bipolar disorder can be dormant for many years and can be caused by its own or caused by external factors like social stress as well as psychological pressure.

Are there any health conditions or illnesses that could co-exist in bipolar disorder?

Other conditions can co-exist in bipolar disorders. Knowing the existence of these co-morbidities is crucial to avoid negative effects. The most frequent conditions associated that are associated with bipolar disorder, is the issue of substance misuse. Teens and adults who suffer from bipolar disorder are at extremely increased chance of developing alcohol or addiction to drugs. It happens when some are prone to binge drinking and using drugs to treat their symptoms. It is crucial to remember that abuse of substances can delay recovery and could cause depressive or manic episodes.

Another disorder that could coexist with bipolar disorder is Attention deficit hyperactivity disorder (ADHD). ADHD is often seen in people who have experienced bipolar symptoms in their early years. Particularly, children who suffer from Bipolar Disorder and ADHD simultaneously have difficulty concentrating and controlling their behavior. They are apparent even when they're not experiencing the typical mood swings that are seen with bipolar disorder.

Anxiety disorders, such as generalized anxiety disorder separation anxiety, generalized anxiety disorder social phobia, and Post-traumatic Stress Disorder (PTSD) are often associated alongside bipolar disorders. This can be seen in both children and adults. People who suffer from bipolar disorder are also at a greater chance of developing heart issues as well as migraine as well as diabetes, obesity, as well as other physical ailments.

The process of diagnosing and treating bipolar disorder is more difficult when there is the existence of these diseases. Therefore, it is essential for those who suspect bipolar disorder to keep track of their mental and the physical condition.

Improvements and changes that occur following treatment must be reported immediately.

How can bipolar disorder affect my life or that of someone who suffers from it?

Bipolar disorder is a disease that usually lasts the span of a life time. Depressive and manic episodes can persist without treatment. Many people remain afflicted after receiving appropriate and consistent treatment.

These are the main types of bipolar disorder.

Bipolar I disorder

Bipolar one disorder defined by the occurrence of mixed episodes of manic and depression lasting for at least one week. It's also characterized by manic-like symptoms that are severe and require immediate hospital treatment. Manic and depressive episodes that occur in this kind of bipolar disorder must be regarded as unusual behavior that is disrupting the life of a person.

Bipolar II disorder

Bipolar II disorder, however, is defined by mood shifts between depressive and hypomanic episodes. Manic episodes, however, in this kind of bipolar disorder don't fully develop into manic or mixed episodes.

Cyclothymia

Cyclothymia can be described as a mild variant that is a mild form of bipolar disorder. Patients diagnosed with it experience periods of hypomania which can change to mild depression, but aren't as prolonged or as long-lasting as complete depression.

Mixed bipolar

Mixed bipolar manifests as episodes that exhibit both symptoms of manic and depression episodes. People who suffer from this kind of bipolar disorder can be emotional, anxious, moody and generally anxious. They also experience grandiose as well as racing thoughts.

Bipolar disorder with rapid cycling

This kind of bipolar disorder manifests itself as frequent mood changes for four or more times in a single year. The episodes should be for a couple of days in order to be considered distinct episodes. The rapid cycling can occur at any time throughout the course of the illness however experts believe it is more common in the latter phases of life. Women are thought to be affected by the rapid bipolar cycling more frequently than males. The rapid cycle pattern can increase suicidal risks and severe depression. Antidepressants used as a treatment strategy is believed to trigger and prolong episodes of rapid cycling.

Bipolar disorder can become more severe if it is not treated prompt and appropriate treatment. People with the disorder suffer more frequent and severe times compared to the time when the symptoms first began to manifest. Inability to recognize it as bipolar disorder may cause patients to have issues with school or job performance. It can significantly hinder one's ability to complete school tasks and to hold the job. It also impacts the social and personal life. So, it is crucial that a timely diagnosis and treatment is taken to ensure that sufferers of bipolar disorder lead happy and healthy lives. This can further assist in decreasing the frequency and severity of its symptoms.

What is the process of diagnosing bipolar disorder?

Bipolar disorder isn't easily recognized. It is often the case that it's mistaken for other disorders like conduct disorders, anxiety disorders, or mood disorders. However, the increased knowledge of mental disorders in the present helped in identifying the signs of bipolar disorder, including hypomania, mania and depression. It is vital to know however that there are no tests in the lab or costly imaging methods can assist in making a correct diagnosis. Instead the bipolar disorder is recognized through a series conversations with a physician regarding mood, behavior and the way of life.

It is a time to take in the history of

A psychiatrist will inquire about the symptoms that a suspect bipolar patient experienced, including the severity, duration of time and when it first started to manifest and if the symptoms were managed. The details of the family's medical background will also be requested. Family members of the patient will also be questioned if it is suspected that the patient is a minor or an adult.

Psychological evaluation

The ideal person to conduct the psychological assessment is psychiatrists. Diagnoses of bipolar disorder are determined by the data collected from the history-taking. The evaluation could include mental health tests to determine whether interpersonal relationships, reasoning speech patterns and memory are affected, which could be caused by bipolar disorder. The psychiatrist could also assess the patient's symptoms for other mental health problems to rule out the possibility of other illnesses.

Charting moods

The doctor may inquire of the bipolar patient suspected to record and keep an account of each day's moods, sleeping patterns, and other vital elements that can aid in diagnosing the bipolar disorder.

Physical exam

A general practitioner will conduct a physical examination to determine the cause of abrupt mood swings (e.g. hypothyroidism). Tests for hypothyroidism will be conducted and, if the cause is physical eliminated, the patient will be referred to an mental health professional for further evaluation.

What is the treatment for bipolar disorder?

Bipolar disorder can have a significant impact on the lives of individuals. It can cause damage to relationships and careers, and could even cause suicide. There is no cure, but it is treatable. The right treatment can be extremely helpful in reducing mood swings along with other signs. Treatment typically includes long-term psychotherapy as well as medication used to ensure a complete control over the symptoms and avoid repetition of depressive and manic episodes.

Medicines

The medications used to treat bipolar disorder require prescriptions from mental health professionals , including psychiatrists and psychiatric nurse specialists as well as clinical psychologists. It is crucial to remember that not all people respond to these medications in the same manner. You may have to try different drugs before settling on the most effective method of solution. Maintaining a daily log of moods, intake of medication and any side effects that occur will help monitor the progression of disease as well as determining the most effective treatment for every patient. The most commonly used medicines and the adverse negative effects will be listed here.

Lithium

Lithium is also known under the brand terms Lithobid as well as Eskalith is one of the widely prescribed medication to treat bipolar disorder. Recent and earlier studies on the effectiveness of this medication demonstrate that it is able to aid in decreasing the frequency and intensity in manic-related episodes. It can also aid in the treatment of depression and could also reduce suicidal thoughts. Lithium can also help in preventing the recurrence of mood changes; therefore, it is usually recommended as a preventative therapy for prolonged durations of time.

Side effects:

The majority of people who use lithium for bipolar disorders will experience small adverse negative effects. These can be seen in the first few weeks after using the drug. Most of the time, these side symptoms are alleviated with dosage manipulation. It is important to remember that it is essential to speak with a doctor prior to making any changes to the medication prescription. The most frequent adverse effects of lithium include hand tremors and thirstiness and frequent urination and weight growth, acne, diarrhea nausea, fatigue memory issues, trouble in concentration, hair loss and fatigue. Contact your doctor immediately in the event of slurred or slurred speaking or fever, diarrhea and unsteady gait. You may also experience weak heartbeat, fainting or confusion.

Conclusion

Bipolar disorder can be a self-destructing, and even fatal illness. This is precisely what the legal system demands to define as a mental disorder that puts the patient at risk to themselves as well as to other people. If you fail to take care of your illness, it will require you to be voluntarily committed to a proper institution in accordance with the law stipulates. Why should you be subject to this, even if you have a tangible and effective solution?

A final piece of advice:

The desire to improve your health has an important element to it. It is essential to take action, and convince yourself that it can work. It's not going to succeed if you constantly tell yourself "I would like to improve however nothing will work on my behalf". This is a reason to say the least.

Never think "what's the point for it?"

Do not think about whether you'll improve your health.

Do not think about WHEN you'll improve.

Remind yourself constantly that "I will improve! Every day!" That is the method to overcome bipolar disorder. You will improve.